To Dean, Susan and Adrian

TABLE OF CONTENTS

Acknowledgments

We are grateful to many people for their assistance in the preparation of this book, especially to the National Park Service staff members who shared their written material, guided us at the seashores, answered hundreds of questions, and read and commented on early drafts of the manuscript. Particularly, we want to thank Barbara Payne of the National Park Service Public Inquiries office in Washington D.C., National Seashores Superintendents Jack Hauptman at Fire Island, Mack Riddel at Cape Lookout, Ken Morganat Cumberland Island, Art Graham at Canaveral, and Jerry Eubanks at Gulf Islands National Seashores and staff members Frank Ackerman at Cape Cod, Neal Bullington at Fire Island, Larry Points at Assateague Island, Bob Woody at Cape Hatteras, Mary Jones at Gulf Islands, Bob Whistler at Padre Island, and Dave Pugh and Don Neubergher at Point Reyes National Seashores. The nation is truly fortunate to have such capable, dedicated, and cooperative public servants.

We Americans would not have ten beautiful national seashores in which to indulge our favorite forms of seashore recreation if it were not for the many thousands of private citizens who, year after year, put their considerable energies to the task of finding ways to preserve large sections of undeveloped shoreline as a national heritage that could be known and enjoyed by future generations. Some are still working to achieve the difficult balance between preservation and active recreation as members of advisory commissions and as volunteers in numerous seashore activities and programs. We were fortunate to meet some of these citizens. We'd particularly like to thank Jim Stevens, who shared with us his records and his memories about the campaign to "Save the Fort" at Ship

Island, Mississippi, David Stick of Kitty Hawk, North
Carolina, whose outstanding writing talents have helped
to further public knowledge of the unique history and
resources of Cape Hatteras, Sherill Smith at Cape Cod,
who educated us in the contribution of advisory commissions to the successful joining of seashore and local interests, and Nancy Butler, whose personal recollections of life
on Cumberland Island before the National Seashore were
a delight to hear.

Finally, our deep appreciation goes to Dr. Stephen P.
Leatherman of the University of Maryland, who gracious-
ly agreed to review the last chapter of this book and granted
us permission to use material from his *Barrier Island Handbook.*

Foreword

AMERICA'S NATIONAL SEASHORES. What are they? Where are they? Why are they so special?

America's national seashores are ten federally-administered coastal parks that include wide stretches of sand beaches, towering sand dunes, rich marshlands, lush maritime forests, quiet ponds, historic sites, and magnificent scenery.

Seven of these seashores are on the Atlantic Coast; two border the Gulf of Mexico; and one, far different from the rest, juts out into the Pacific Ocean.

People can swim, collect shells, hike, fish, hunt, boat, and camp at the national seashores, just as they can at other ocean beaches. But, unlike beaches open only to a restricted group of people, these seashores are set aside by law for everyone's pleasure. Future generations will be able to enjoy them, just as their parents and grandparents did, because their splendid resources are being carefully safeguarded. Some provide recreation for masses of people at one time; some offer the chance to enjoy the solitude of lone beach walking, backcountry hiking, or primitive camping.

As we recall our several months' journey to all the national seashores, a few vignettes come to mind:

- the lone beach stroller on Nauset Beach, Cape Cod National Seashore in Massachusetts, bundled up in boots, quilted jacket, wool scarf and fur hat on a sunny but windy 30 degree day in January;

- the young mother on the ferryboat to Cumberland Island National Seashore in Georgia, carrying plastic sand toys for her three year old as well as camp tools on her backpack;

- the three fishermen on the remote Core Banks of Cape Lookout National Seashore in North Carolina, casting a net into the water to catch bait and hopping into a jeep to drive down the beach to a favorite fishing spot;

- a middle-aged twosome on a platform overlooking a pond teeming with wildfowl at Cape Hatteras National Seashore in North Carolina, peering intently through binoculars, excitedly claiming a new bird to add to their "life list."

We visited the national seashores in winter, spring, summer, and fall. We walked the beaches and nature trails, took boats to the off-shore islands, visited historic structures, and peered at seldom-seen wildlife.

What we saw and heard brought a lift to our spirits. We are sharing what we discovered so that others may know the great variety of pleasurable experiences awaiting them at our national seashores.

We found out something else during our visits. National seashores not only provide seaside recreation for millions of people; they also are maritime proving grounds. Most national seashores are on barrier islands—coastal islands that serve as a buffer for the American mainland from the onslaughts of a powerful sea. The sands, waters, and vegetation of barrier islands have a special relationship created by nature. Sometimes man interferes with that relationship. At the national seashores we are learning how man can use and enjoy island resources, but also adapt to the forces of "that old devil sea."

The last chapter of this book is intended to augment the reader's beach pleasures with an understanding of what is happening on the nation's barrier islands. And it alerts us to the choices that will soon have to be made about how these islands are to be used in the years to come.

So go to the beaches—enjoy the fun, sun, cool breezes, close encounters with nature—whatever you seek. But, if you love the beach, we hope you will also take time to reflect on these treasured resources and help decide what sort of beach environment our generation will bequeath to the shore lovers of the future.

The National Seashores

Today's Pleasures — Tomorrow's Inheritance

Our national seashores include islands, peninsulas, and nearby mainland sites that Congress has established as units of the National Park System to be administered for the benefit and enjoyment of all people. Most seashores have entrance or parking fees, but once there, there is no charge to walk on the beach, bask in the sun, surfcast, or ride a rolling wave. Anyone who wants to can walk the nature trails or view historic lighthouses.

The only requirement is a willingness to abide by a few regulations established to protect the natural—and, in some instances, man-made—environments.

There are ten national seashores, all but one on the Atlantic or Gulf coasts. Some, like Fire Island in New York, Cape Cod in Massachusetts, and Cape Hatteras in North Carolina, are near large cities and almost everyone has heard of them. Others are not so well known.

How It All Started

When there are thousands of miles of coastline and hundreds of islands on the Atlantic, Gulf of Mexico, and Pacific coasts, how did these particular places come to be designated *national seashores?*

It all happened within the space of a few years. Well, not *all*. Behind each national seashore lies a story of hard work, over many years, by dedicated seashore lovers. There came a time, however, from the mid-fifties to the mid-seventies, when a number of motivating forces came together.

Starting with the 1930s, an increasing number of our leaders began to recognize outdoor recreation as an activity to be fostered. People in cities and towns were traveling in greater numbers to the mountains and to the shore, seeking a refreshing change from their normal environment. At the same time, interest in protecting the nation's diminishing natural resources was accelerating; more often than not, this interest focused on the same sites that were being eyed by real estate developers. Out of these converging forces came the first in a series of national seashores.

At Cape Hatteras, North Carolina, in the early thirties, a group of civic leaders put together a concern about beach erosion on the one hand and the island's weak Depression-era economy on the other, to build a movement for a "National Coastal Park." The campaign, coinciding with a federal government interest in acquiring more park land, culminated in 1937 with the passage of the first law authorizing the creation of a national seashore. But it takes more than a law on the books to make a national seashore. The federal government at that time could only acquire seashore land by donation or by purchase with donated funds. It wasn't until 1953 that the national seashore became a reality.

The idea of making Assateague Island off the Maryland and Virginia coasts, a national seashore first surfaced in a 1935 survey of lands on the Atlantic and Gulf coasts. Congressional interest waxed and waned and in the early fifties developers stepped into the picture. Land was acquired and subdivided, a road built and a publicity blitz launched to sell lots for vacation retreats. Then in March 1962, a storm devastated the island. Vacation home development no longer seemed appealing. Interest in a federal seashore was rekindled, and in 1965, the bill making Assateague Island a national seashore became a law.

The spark that led to the creation of the Gulf Islands National Seashore was the "never say die" attitude of a group of Gulf Shore citizens in Mississippi. For many years they had been trying to save an historic fort on an island twelve miles off shore from devastation by wind and wave. While some volunteers conducted a holding operation, others tried to interest city, county, and state governments in the project. There were no takers. Finally, with the help of congressional leaders, they joined forces with civic leaders in Pensacola, Florida, who were also trying to save the historic coastal forts of their area. Success came in 1971 when six islands spanning a 150-mile coastline were linked to form Gulf Islands National Seashore.

The Seashore Movement Picks Up Steam

In the twenty-two years after Cape Hatteras officially became a national seashore, laws were passed authorizing all the other seashores. In addition to Cape Hatteras, Assateague Island, and Gulf Islands National Seashores, there now are:

- Cape Cod in Massachusetts, authorized in 1961
- Point Reyes in California, 1962
- Padre Island in Texas, 1962
- Fire Island in New York, 1964
- Cape Lookout in North Carolina, 1966
- Cumberland Island in Georgia, 1972

- Canaveral in Florida, 1975

During the same period, spurred by the growing environmental movement, Congress passed laws to protect the nation's resources—land, water, fish, wildlife, plants, and historical. These laws today determine to a great extent the way national seashores and other lands within the National Park System are administered. (See the end of this chapter for a summary of some of these laws.)

Seashores Are Not All The Same

Seashores vary in size from the 19,579 acres of Seashore Beach spotted among seventeen communities on Fire Island to the 139,775 acres of islands, mainland sites, and adjacent waters that make up Gulf Islands National Seashore. Cape Cod and Gulf Islands have the most visitors. Miles and miles of magnificent beaches, famous historical sites, and easy auto access attract nearly twelve million people a year to these two national seashores alone. They are surrounded by towns and villages bursting with private motel/hotel accommodations, restaurants of all sorts, and entertainment facilities.

At the other end of the scale, Cumberland Island and Cape Lookout are the most remote seashores in the system. In 1986, 29,000 people visited Cumberland Island and 98,000 went to Cape Lookout. These seashores can be reached only by private boat or by ferry at rates varying from $6.25 to $40.00 and no services of any kind are provided.

Conflicts And Costs

Millions of tax dollars are spent to run the ten national seashores. Sometimes taxpayers question why they can't do as they please at national parks—hunt, ride bikes, drive beach buggies, build fires, camp—whatever they want.

But it's not so simple. There are conflicts and costs. First, the conflicts. National seashores must, by law, provide for public enjoyment of "unique natural, historic and scientific features" and "preserve for future generations . . . unspoiled and undeveloped beaches, dunes and other natural features." At the same time, seashores must "develop for appropriate use" facilities for camping, swimming, boating, hunting, and fishing.

The beauty of a landscape, along with thoughts on how to enjoy it, varies with the eye and personal inclination of the beholder. Picture three persons standing at the water's edge on an unoccupied beach. One is buoyed by the prospect of taking a solitary walk on an undeveloped beach—just as nature has formed it. Another excitedly plans for a great beach party for her friends, complete with blaring music, volleyball, roaring fire, and stimulating drink. A third sees it as an open road for his dune buggy to get him to a better fishing spot.

Balancing all these interests in the use of the beach, and the maritime forests, marshes, and bay waters of a national seashore is the responsibility of national seashore policy-makers and the staff assigned to carry out their decisions. It is no easy task.

There are the beach users with their conflicting interests. There are environmental activists with strong preservation views. And there is yet another force to be reckoned with—nature in the form of wind, tides, waves, and sea creatures whose lives depend on natural interaction of sand and water. How these conflicting interests are resolved must be guided by scientific study of the effect of different kinds of human activity on the various natural features of the seashores.

National seashores aren't all managed alike. At some, four-wheel drive vehicles (ORVs)[1] are allowed on the beach; at others, they aren't. Some have strict regulations about walking through the dunes; others don't. Some maintain heavily-used paved roads; others let washed-out roads return to a natural state.

A number of factors affect such decisions: the expressed intent of the law creating the seashore, traditional uses of the beach by local residents, the vigor with which citizen groups express their opinions, and the condition of the particular natural resource in question.

Now, the costs. The axiom, "You don't get something for nothing," applies to seashores as much as to everything else. Costs may be in the form of activities prohibited. Dune buggies may be forbidden in certain areas to protect fragile sand dunes from unnatural disturbances—or, at times, to allow endangered sea turtles or terns to carry on their normal life cycles. Access to some areas may be restricted because of the damaging effects of heavy visitor usage.

Costs can also mean the payment of a modest parking or campground usage fee, and sometimes a sizable fee to ride a ferryboat to an offshore island, when that is the only way to get there.

Past park service policy has been to keep the costs of enjoying national parks to a minimum, making it possible for all citizens, no matter the size of their purses, to enjoy the parks. For $10.00 a person could buy a Golden Eagle passport, allowing free entrance to all national parks for a year. Persons sixty-two or over have been able to get a Golden Age passport and persons who have been medically determined to be blind or disabled and eligible for benefits under federal law could obtain a Golden Access passport. Golden Age and Golden Access passports provide free

---

[1] Off-road vehicles, also called oversand vehicles or dune buggies.

lifetime access to all national parks where there is an entrance fee and discounts on fee-paid facilities.

The policy appears to be coming to an end. In 1987, entrance fees were imposed at many parks where there used to be none. Golden Age and Golden Access passports are still free, but the cost of the Golden Eagle passport has gone up to $25.00.

There are several reasons for this change. The federal budget is being squeezed in a time of deficits. There is a growing belief that those who use federal services, including parks, should pay a larger share of the cost of their maintenance. It's also felt by some that imposing or raising fees will cut down on visitor usage in areas threatened by their own popularity.

Managing National Seashores; Or A Place For Everything

People who enjoy going to the seashore—for whatever reason—want to go back. They want to swim, fish, surf, hike, or camp in their favorite spots again. But a seashore never stays the same. It is constantly changing. A storm alters the shape of the beach or creates a new inlet. Raccoons destroy turtle nests. An old life-saving station is vandalized. Water inundates a campground. Litter appears on a trail through a maritime forest.

As custodians of all lands, waters, and structures of the seashores, rangers and other staff work to keep national seashores places that beachgoers will enjoy returning to for years to come. But whether they succeed in their efforts depends not only on adequate staff and money, but ultimately on the cooperation of the beach user.

Cooperation usually comes with understanding and good will. Most beach visitors bring their good will with them when they first arrive on seashore property. Not all, however, understand the reason for certain rules and regulations. An explanation of how decisions are made about the use of seashore resources may help.

Every seashore administration prepares a plan for managing its responsibilities. Some of the plans are several years in the making. Everyone gets a say before a plan is jelled—the general public, persons representing recreation and environmental interests, governments, federal, state, and local. Proposed actions are sometimes the center of great controversy. When this is the case, public meetings are held and, after all concerns are expressed, an attempt is made to find a meeting of the minds.

Some national seashores have advisory commissions that include representatives of state and local governments and the public. They often play an important role in seeing that local interests are taken into consideration when seashore policies are set.

In carrying out their responsibility to balance the many national interests, seashore staff analyze each plot of ground and body of water to determine what sort of activity is appropriate for that area. Each is then placed in one of several "management zones." Here is what can happen on lands and water in each zone.

Natural Zone Shores, dunes, forests, trails, ponds, and bays placed in this category are managed so as to keep them as much as possible in their natural state. Only human activity that will have a minimum impact on the natural processes is permitted. There is no development beyond possibly sparsely-located picnic facilities and interpretive displays that foster appreciation of the surrounding resources. *Example:* signs identifying indigenous plants along a trail in the Sunken Forest of Fire Island National Seashore and along the Grasslands Trail of Padre Island National Seashore.

Historic Zone Lands are placed in this category primarily to preserve significant cultural resources and historic sites. Only activities that serve that purpose, which includes explanations of their significance, takes place. *Example:* Fort Barrancas in Pensacola, Gulf Islands National Seashore, and the Cape Hatteras Lighthouse.

Park Development These areas are designated for the location of facilities necessary to the support of intensive public use. *Example:* parking lots, roads, and utilities.

Development Zone Major facilities and lands set aside for intensive public use are located in this zone. *Example:* life-guarded beaches, day-use services provided by concessionaires, campgrounds, and heavily used visitor centers.

Occasionally the seashore designates certain lands and waters within its boundaries as "special use" sites. These are places used for non-seashore purposes. *Example:* Coast Guard stations, local government utilities, or privately-run commercial facilities such as overseas communication towers.

Other "Interested Parties"

In addition to the people who go to the beach for recreational pursuits and the environmentalists and maritime scientists who have a national policy interest in seashore actions, there are other groups with a stake in how national seashores are run.

Enacting a law authorizing creation of a national seashore does not automatically make the designated land and waters a possession of the federal government. At first, there is only a map defining boundaries and language expressing intentions. Land must be acquired by various means. The preferred method is donation, usually of state-owned land or land owned by nonprofit organizations that bought them originally to forestall threatened development. Other lands may be added through exchange of surplus federally-owned land or land owned by other government units.

The Private Landholder When funds are available, the federal government buys land that is privately-owned or, as a last resort, it is obtained by condemnation, with courts determining the fair market price.

Very often the terms negotiated for the purchase of privately-owned land permit the owner—and sometimes the heirs—to remain in the home for a specified length of time before it eventually becomes public property. Certain restrictions on the owner's use of the land in the interim apply. Here and there a seashore visitor will see signs asking people to respect the rights of private individuals living on seashore property.

Commercial Interests National seashores often surround villages and towns, and seashores try to be good neighbors. Seashores build no more roads or camping facilities than absolutely necessary. Local businesses in nearby towns usually offer an array of overnight accommodations, food, and other services. Some seashores arrange for concessionaires to provide lunch or snack food or transportation to and within park boundaries.

Other Government Entities All government activities are conducted "in the public interest." And each government that has jurisdiction in or near a national seashore considers itself the guardian of the public interest. This situation can lead to conflicts and the need to "work things out."

Federal agencies that frequently conduct activities within national seashores include the U.S. Coast Guard, the Army Corps of Engineers, and the Fish and Wildlife Service. At Canaveral National Seashore, the National Aeronautics and Space Administration (NASA) has the authority to limit seashore activity at times when space launches and landings take place.

Seashore staff often consult with such state government authorities as historic preservation officers, environmental policy officers, and administrators of adjacent state parks about their mutual interests. They also work with local law enforcement, environmental control, and zoning authorities to ensure that the concerns of both governments are taken into consideration when their interests overlap.

Seashore Boosters National seashores, like other components of the National Park System, have their boosters—people and organizations that play a direct but little-known role in the support of the seashores. Volunteers, some working under the National Volunteers in Parks program, plant beach grass to help stabilize dunes, clean up beaches and roadways, help lay out nature trails, staff information booths and campgrounds, participate in research programs, and use photographic and other skills to fill needs that can't be met from a limited budget.

Nonprofit organizations such as the National Park Foundation and The Nature Conservancy have sought out and bought land for subsequent donation to the National Park System, including the seashores.

The National Park Foundation, which is chartered by Congress, also uses funds obtained by contributions, grants, and special government appropriations to perform certain services for the seashores such as repairing, refurbishing, or replacing visitor facilities. From privately-raised money, the foundation funds special visitor information projects.

Almost from the beginning of the National Park Service in 1917, citizens formed numerous "cooperating associations" to spread the word about the national parks. These organizations publish inexpensive leaflets and other interpretive literature, donate equipment for environmental education programs, and help fund research efforts. Those working to enhance national seashore programs include: Coastal Parks Association, associated with Point Reyes National Seashore; Eastern National Park and Monument Association, which assists Assateague Island, Canaveral, Cape Cod, Cape Hatteras, Cape Lookout, Cumberland Island, Fire Island and Gulf Island National Seashores; and Southwest Parks and Monument Association, a supporter of Padre Island National Seashore.

The National Parks and Conservation Association, an organization with 55,000 members nationwide, is dedicated to the preservation and enhancement of the National Park System and is completely independent of the National Park Service. It keeps a watchful eye on legislative and administrative actions affecting national parks and doesn't hesitate to praise, condemn, or suggest ways to improve park administration. It conducts an active program to mobilize citizens in support of its efforts. Among its recent activities has been sponsorship of research to devise a scientifically sound method for managing the impact of recreational activities on the natural environs of parks—seashores included.

The chapters that follow discuss the historical background, special attributes, and specific regulations of each of the ten national seashores. However a few park service operating policies apply to all seashores:

- Picking of sea grasses and other forms of live vegetation growing in the dunes or forests is strictly prohibited. Visitors may gather seashells for noncommercial purposes as long as there are no live creatures within and they may pick edible berries.

- No metal detectors may be used on the beaches or elsewhere. This is to avoid disturbance to possible cultural, historical, or archeological resources.

- Pets are not allowed in specified areas. In places where they are permitted, they must be under physical control at all times. This usually means on leashes no longer than six feet.

- Most seashores have special facilities for the physically impaired. Where they do not exist, such as on ferries to off-shore islands, it may be possible for the seashore administration to make special arrangements if contacted in advance.

Some Of The Laws Governing How National Seashores Are Administered

The National Wilderness Act (1964) This act established a wilderness category for federally-owned land and defined such land as "an area where the earth and its community of life are untrammeled by man, where man himself is a visitor who does not remain." To qualify for this designation, land must retain "its primeval character and influence, without permanent improvements or human habitation." It must "generally appear to have been affected primarily by the forces of nature, with the imprint of man's work substantially unnoticeable." There are wilderness areas in Fire Island, Gulf Islands, Cumberland Island, and Point Reyes National Seashores.

The Land And Water Conservation Act (1954) This act recognized the importance of outdoor recreation activity "to strengthen the health and vitality of American citizens" and set up a special fund for the purchase of land

and waters for recreational purposes. The law particularly encouraged action to provide outdoor recreation near urban centers. It also set up a system of daily, annual, and lifetime admission fees for certain national parks. Assateague Island National Seashore, which is near the city of Baltimore, Maryland, was authorized soon after the law went into effect.

The National Historic Preservation Act (1966) This act provided for maintenance of a National Register of Historic Places. A process was established for placing on the register certain historical districts, sites, buildings, structures, and objects significant in American history, architecture, archeology, and culture. Among national seashore places now on the National Register are several lighthouses, historic forts, an Indian midden, early maritime farms and houses, shipwreck sites, and a camp for ranch workers.

The Volunteers In Parks Act (1970) This act set up a program in which trained volunteers can help to manage and operate national parks by providing visitor information, patrolling backcountry areas, and helping with wildlife and timber management, and other park activities. In 1986, some 26,000 volunteers worked at national parks, including national seashores, performing services valued at over nine million dollars.

The Endangered Species Act (1973) This act expressed national concern about the increasing extinction of various species of fish, wildlife, and plants. Recognizing that economic growth and development often threaten other species of esthetic, ecological, educational, historical, recreational, and scientific value, the law set up a program for saving them. Many mammals, birds, reptiles, and plants found at the national seashores are on the lists of endangered species or endangered plants.

Cape Cod National Seashore

"A man may stand there and put all America behind him."

— *Henry David Thoreau*

A person can *still* stand alone on the sandy cliffs of Cape Cod, look out at the ocean and feel like an adventurer who has discovered America's frontier with the sea. For the peninsula that is Cape Cod juts farther out into the Atlantic Ocean than any other piece of land in the United States.

For nearly 400 years, Americans and their European forefathers have been drawn to this aptly-termed coastal "arm," formed by a series of catastrophic geologic actions that began two or three million years ago. Advances and retreats of glaciers alternately covered, then exposed, eastern coastal plains. In the process, Cape Cod's high ridges of rubble and debris, called moraines, were built; great cavities in the land, called kettle holes, now filled with fresh water lakes and ponds, were formed; and, in the adjacent waters, enormous "banks" of glacial remnants were submerged by rising seas.

Visitors to Cape Cod National Seashore can be eyewitnesses to the tugging of land and sea, ever in conflict, that has been going on for centuries and, according to geologists, will continue until at some distant age, the sea will wear down the cliffs and cross the plains and only a few sandy islands will be left.

But for now, all that is great and wonderful about a seashore can be experienced at Cape Cod. Long before there was a national seashore, New Englanders annually went "down to the Cape" to loll on the beach, swim in the surf, sail and fish in the waters, hunt in the marshes and fields, hold clambakes on the shore, and generally recharge their personal batteries. Some owned vacation cottages; many more rented them.

Artists, writers, and craftsmen came, stimulated by the scenic splendor of beaches, dunes, marshes, ocean, boat-filled harbors, abundant bird life, and the "be yourself" attitude of native Cape Codders.

Provincetown, at the tip of the Cape, where in 1899 Charles W. Hawthorne had founded the Cape Cod School of Art, became the center of a famous art colony attracting such painters as Edwin Dickerson, John Nolte, and Jackson Pollack. John Dos Passos, Mary Heaton, and Max Eastman were among the writers who found inspiration at the Cape.

Summer theater groups flourished. Kurt Vonnegut, Basil Rathbone, Bette Davis, Ethel Barrymore, Humphrey Bogart, and Orson Welles are some of the stars of theater and motion pictures whose early careers included performances on Cape Cod.

Most visitors came in the summer. A few, desiring intimate contact with land and sea and the creatures sustained by their interaction, stayed throughout the seasons. Two of these visitors, Henry Beston and Wyman Richardson, recorded their observations and experiences and produced books that are on every Cape lover's "must" reading list.

There came a time in the late 1950s when both year-round residents and people who had already discovered the joys of a visit to Cape Cod realized that the special qualities of the Cape were being threatened by its increasing popularity. There followed nearly three years of painstaking efforts to work out a solution to the dilemma with local residents, accustomed to full participation in town meeting decisions, sharing in the shaping of legislation that led to the establishment of the Cape Cod National Seashore.

Today, Cape Cod National Seashore, within a day's travel of a third of the nation's people, is the most popular seashore on the East Coast. The boundaries of the seashore include over 43,000 acres of the outermost part of the Cape, generally referred to as "the lower Cape."

Following his series of walks on these shores, Henry David Thoreau described Cape Cod as "the bared and bended arm of Massachusetts." The entire shoreline of the Atlantic Ocean from Chatham, where the elbow of the arm bends northward, and along the forearm to around the fist to Cape Cod Bay, about thirty-nine miles, is within the seashore. The beach area is commonly referred to as "The Great Beach."

With the exception of Provincetown on Provincetown Harbor and a small amount of adjacent land, the seashore includes the entire tip of the Cape. About halfway from elbow to fist, within the towns of Truro and Wellfleet, the seashore extends from ocean to bay and includes Great Island, which is now a sandy spit separating Wellfleet Harbor from Cape Cod Bay.

The National Park Service's dual responsibilities to preserve the rich natural, historical, and cultural resources of America, while at the same time providing a variety of top-notch seashore recreational opportunities to masses of people, is constantly being put to the test at Cape Cod.

The seashore was the first national park established in a widespread area in which Americans and their European ancestors had continuously lived, worked, thrived, and developed a considerably independent way of life for over 300 years. Its historical and cultural heritage is known nationwide: here is where the Pilgrims first set foot on American soil, where the first transoceanic transmission of a message from North America over Marconi's wireless originated, where famous shipwrecks and rescues occurred, and where an indigenous housing style developed.

For over a hundred years artists and writers have been extolling Cape Cod's natural beauty and relating tales of its people. It was, and continues to be, a significant challenge to keep this tradition from being buried under the pressures of accommodating the recreational needs of today's urban-centered culture.

Cape Cod Before The National Seashore

Perhaps as long as 10,000 years ago, before the Vikings, European fishermen, explorers, and Pilgrims came upon Cape Cod, Native Americans pursued a nomadic way of life there, hunting and fishing, and gathering fruits and nuts to sustain themselves. By the time the English came in the late 1500s, various subtribes of the Wampanoags had settled along creeks, marshes, and the bay, and were living in primitive houses and cultivating corn, beans, and other crops. Some of the tribes had names now familiar to any Cape visitor—Pamets, Nausets, and Monomoyicks.

Of the many explorers, two were of special significance to Cape Cod. Various Europeans gave names to the area, but it was Bartholomew Gosnold's choice of Cape Cod, for the rich harvest of codfish he found in the bay waters, that lasted.

John Smith's extensive accounts and maps of the New England coast, including the bay side of Cape Cod, were used by the Pilgrims when they turned north after stormy weather forced them to abandon the southerly course they had originally set. They anchored their ship, the *Mayflower*, around the bend of the Cape's tip in Provincetown Harbor in early November 1620.

After 30 days of exploration of the surrounding land and waters, they decided to sail west and settled at Plymouth. Eventually some of their number trekked overland to the Cape to make their homes there and become the ancestors of many of today's Cape Codders. Several place names on Cape Cod commemorate the visit of these early English wayfarers—Pilgrim Heights, Pilgrim Lake, Pilgrim Spring Trail, First Encounter Beach.

The farmers from the Old World soon learned to become fishermen in the New. In the beginning they cleared the land of the vast stands of beech, maple, oak, sassafras, and pine trees, and planted their crops. But when sands began to migrate and harvests were limited, they turned to the sea. There appeared to be an unending supply of lobster, cod, oysters, clams, scallops, and other fish in the adjacent waters. Cape Codders developed a skill for open ocean fishing, a tradition that continues to be an important part of the fabric of Cape Cod.

In the heyday of the whaling industry, Cape Cod seamen pursued their fortunes far away in the waters of the South Pacific and Arctic Oceans and returned home to build impressive houses reflecting a worldliness unusual for the Cape. One of them, the Captain Edward Penniman House, is on seashore property, beautifully preserved and open to visitors at certain times.

The rugged, independent men and women who put their roots down on Cape Cod knew the land and the sea, and they learned to adjust to changes wrought by the ocean's mighty assaults. When they built lighthouses, they knew that in a predictable number of years, they would have to be moved to keep them from falling into the sea. They observed that while the outer cliffs were being severely eroded, the southern and western shores were growing. When they set about to aid shipwrecked sailors, they gauged rescue possibilities by the direction of the wind and its effect on the building of the sandbars.

For nearly three centuries until the Cape Cod Canal opened in 1914, ships sailing south from the North Atlantic had to navigate the dangerous shoals bordering Cape Cod. It's said that over 3,000 ships were lost here, many within sight of people on shore.

No matter what the ship's home port was, Cape Codders felt the loss of every vessel and they gave comfort and assistance to the survivors. Practical people, they also congregated on the beach when wrecked cargo washed ashore and appropriated useful items to fill their own needs.

A series of lighthouses was built, starting in 1797 when the first Highland (Cape Cod) Light was constructed on the high cliffs of Truro. There are many absorbing stories about the lonely vigils of the lighthouse keepers on Cape Cod as over the years they faithfully lit their lamps with whale oil, then kerosene, and finally electricity to guide coastal seafarers. Five lighthouses, now maintained by the U.S. Coast Guard, still stand within seashore territory, picturesque sentinels of the past: Nauset, Highland, Race Point, Wood End, and Long Point.

But lighthouses couldn't prevent all shipwrecks and Cape Codders manned the thirteen stations of the famed U.S. Life-Saving Service, scattered along the shores of the Great Beach. Old Harbor Life-Saving Station, the last survivor of these bases of heroic action, now located on Race Point Beach, is open to visitors, including the physically disabled.

With the completion of the railroad in 1873 and later the building of a road down the center of the Cape and bridges across the Cape Cod Canal, the outer region of Cape Cod became more accessible and vacationers began to flock there. Twentieth century tourism brought prosperity and people took paying guests into their homes, built rental cottages and motels, and opened seasonal restaurants and shops.

The Making Of The Cape Cod National Seashore

Rumors about the federal government's interest in creating a national park on the shores of Cape Cod had been circulating for months by the time the National Park Service invited the residents of the six towns of the lower Cape to public meetings on March 23 and 24, 1959.

After all, a report of a National Park Service Recreation Survey, released in early 1956, had cited the Great Beach at Cape Cod as a top priority for federal action. *The Cape Codder,* a local weekly newspaper, had frequently reported on the National Park Service's interest and state and local officials had been meeting with park service staff to talk about the proposal. A park service surveying team had spent over a year researching all aspects—biological, geological, archeological, historical, and scenic. Legislation to provide for such a park had been introduced in the House of Representatives by three of Massachusetts' Congressmen and it was known that the Governor and the Massachusetts legislature favored the idea.

But the tenacious, independent spirit of the people of Cape Cod had to be contended with. Strong opinions, pro and con, were already held but the townspeople were willing to hear the park service out and were eager to ask questions relating to their concerns. They wanted to know what would happen to their homes and their land and how a national park would affect the economy of their towns.

From then on, the benefit of public participation in the making of government decisions was clear. Over the next two and one-half years, under the bipartisan guidance of Republican Senator Leverett Saltonstall and Democratic Senator John F. Kennedy, legislation was carefully crafted that accommodated the concerns of Cape Cod townspeople, fashioned new ways of doing things by the federal government, and set aside a magnificent shore for all to enjoy.

Perhaps a part of Senator Saltonstall's statement to the congressional committee considering the proposed legislation sums up the motivating factor on which all parties to this landmark effort could agree:

> *As our society grows, the responsibility of Government to preserve certain untouched areas of our country's glorious natural beauty increases. As our cities and suburbs spread, as the invasion of asphalt and harsh neon glare continues, as the smoke and grime of our industries multiply, this obligation for the future becomes more and more pressing. Rapid commercialization must be stopped from destroying the original beauty of an irreplaceable part of America's heritage . . .*

> *We cannot advocate "preservation" in a vacuum. We hope to keep the Cape largely the way it is in order that the people who live there now can continue to enjoy it and so that other Americans, in dire need of the natural grandeur of the clean, open spaces, will find an outlet from their crowded, grimy, urban lives. "Recreation" merely enables people to share the park's refreshing beauty. This dedication to the spiritual replenishment of modern man is the essence of the whole concept of a park on the Cape.*

Cape Cod was not the first national seashore. That distinction belongs to Cape Hatteras National Seashore. But there were many "firsts" in the Cape Cod legislation that was signed by President Kennedy on August 7, 1961 in his first year in office.

- Congress authorized the National Park Service to use public funds to buy land for a major park. Up until that time, land had to be donated or purchased with donated funds.

- A home within the seashore boundaries that was built before September 1, 1959 could be granted a certificate exempting it forever from federal condemnation, provided the towns adopted zoning regulations satisfactory to the Secretary of the Interior.

- An advisory commission was set up. It consisted of ten members representing the six lower Cape towns (Chatham, Orleans, Eastham, Wellfleet, Truro, and Provincetown), Barnstable County, the Commonwealth of Massachusetts and the U.S. Department of the Interior. For many years the commission played a key role in the development of seashore policies. Its independent spirit and the diligence with which its members approached their tasks caused it to earn the respect of both the seashore management and the local constituency.

Today the seashore and the towns are de facto partners in a continuing effort not only to preserve the Cape's natural, historical, and cultural resources, but also to find practical solutions to the modern-day problems of both the seashore and the local communities. As one local resident put it, the "thumbs down" attitude of local residents who first objected to the seashore has now turned "thumbs up!"

Cape Cod National Seashore Today

Summer, fall, winter, or spring—every season at the Cape Cod National Seashore is a favorite with somebody. It's that kind of place. Beaches, dunes, woodland and marshland trails, birdlife, and ocean views are always there but the variation in form, shade, surface, wind, and temperature ensures a different experience with each season.

Masses of people descend on all of Cape Cod, the peninsula, during the traditional summer vacation period. After slowly wending your way through the built-up towns of the "upper Cape," from the canal to Chatham, you reach the area encompassing the national seashore. If the beach is your destination and you are not there early, you may have a long wait to find a parking space at either the town or seashore beaches. Once there, however, there is room for everyone and summer beach lovers consider the pleasures of sunbathing, swimming, and picnicking on the Great Beach worth the effort.

Fall, with its clear skies, crisp air, fewer visitors, and brilliant hues of deep orange, scarlet, and purple, appeals especially to hikers, bike-riders, and bird-watchers. There is time and space for serious fishing in the surf, hunting in the marshes, beachcombing, scanning the horizon for a gathering of humpback whales, and listening to the sounds of the sea.

"The sea has many voices," Henry Beston tells us in *The Outermost House.*

> *Hollow boomings and heavy roarings, great watery tumblings and tramplings, long hissing seethes, sharp, rifle-shot reports, splashes, whispers, the grinding undertone of stones and sometimes vocal sounds that might be the half-heard talk of people in the sea . . . it is also constantly changing its tempo, its pitch, its ac-*

cent, and its rhythm, being now loud and thundering, now almost placid, now furious, now grave and solemn-slow . . .

Winter on the Cape, with its somewhat milder climate than further inland, has its own special attraction. All the treasures washed in by the sea belong to the lone beach walker. Harbor seals and grey seals can be spotted in the surf searching for food. When the cold winds blow and the heavy rains come, long-time residents are reminded of shipwrecks past and will relate gripping tales and possibly show you some of the ships' remains.

Spring comes late to Cape Cod but many who feel the need to shake the "March Doldrums" as Wyman Richardson describes in *The House on Nauset Marsh*, head for the Cape in search of an antidote, usually found in long walks on trails through woods, around ponds, and along ocean cliffs, observing migrating birds and the early stirrings of nature's creatures.

How To Get There

U.S. Route 6, the mid-Cape highway, runs the entire length of Cape Cod. Well-marked side roads from Route 6 take you to visitor centers, beaches, trails, scenic overlooks, and historical sites. There is such a wealth of places to go it is wise to send in advance or stop at the first seashore visitor center at Salt Pond in Eastham, or at national seashore headquarters in South Wellfleet to get the park service brochure which includes a map showing the location of every facility.

Where To Stay

Private Accommodations The Cape Cod
Chamber of Commerce publishes a resort directory listing
hotels, motels, housekeeping cottages, apartments, condominiums, and Bed and Breakfast facilities all over the
Cape. The resort directory also contains information on
services and commercial attractions such as boat excur-
sions. Due to the summertime influx of vacationers, it is
wise to make reservations for overnight facilities months
in advance if you plan to go to Cape Cod during that
season.

Camping The national seashore does not maintain
campgrounds and no overnight camping on the beach is
permitted. However there are private campgrounds in and
near the park. The Chamber of Commerce Resort Directory includes a list of campgrounds and trailer parks, including addresses and phone numbers. There is also a directory
devoted solely to campgrounds, hostels and trailer parks.

Nickerson State Park, located on Route 6A in Brewster
(Exit 12 from U.S. Route 6), a town on the western side of
Orleans, offers 418 campsites. It is open April 15 to October
15 on a first come, first served basis. There are no trailer
hook-ups.

What To Do At Cape Cod

The Visitor Center A good way for the first-time
visitor to start his Cape Cod experience is to stop at either
or both of the two seashore visitor centers: Salt Pond
Visitor Center on Route 6 at Eastham and Province Lands
Visitor Center on Race Point Road near Provincetown.
They are open 9 a.m. to 6 p.m. in the summer, until 4:30

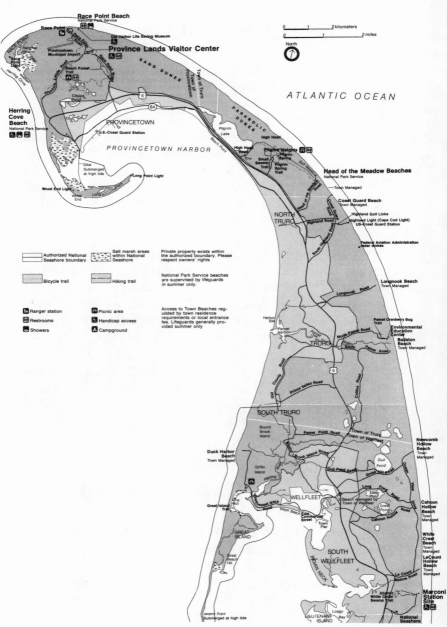

Continued on next page

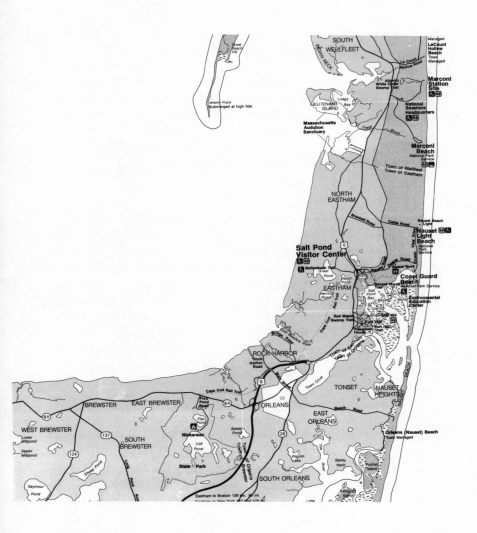

p.m. at other times. Province Lands is closed from December to mid-April and Salt Pond is closed during January and February. During these months, information and publications can be obtained at seashore headquarters in South Wellfleet.

Both visitor centers show films about the seashore and offer exhibits and publications. Information on walking, bicycling, and horseback riding trails and about the various provisions made for disabled visitors, including the visual and hearing impaired, to enjoy the park can be obtained at the centers. In the summer and fall, you can pick up a schedule of ranger-led activities.

The Beaches   In summer the seashore maintains the following lifeguarded beaches: Coast Guard, Nauset Light, Marconi, Head of the Meadow, Race Point, and Herring Cove. Special areas are designated for surfers. Several of the towns own beaches within the boundaries of the seashore and they are open to the public also. All developed beaches charge entrance fees during the season of heavy use. The fee paid at Coast Guard beach includes the use of shuttle transportation from the parking area, located opposite Doane Rock, one of the seashore's geologic attractions.

The Trails   Spend some time walking on some of the seashore's ten well-maintained trails along marshes, through swamps and forests and to historic areas. Some are short walks—like the trail to the ocean cliffs where Guglielmo Marconi set up his great towers and in 1903 President Theodore Roosevelt and King Edward VII of England exchanged the first transoceanic messages. So is the trail leading to the spring at which the Pilgrims are said to have taken their first drink of water on American soil. Others—along the Nauset Marsh or through the White Cedar Swamp or the Beech Forest—are about a mile long. The experienced walker will enjoy the isolated Great Island Trail, a 5.5 mile hike. Trails have trailside labels. Brochures providing information about what you see, hear, or smell may be picked up at trailside boxes as you start your walk. Markers along the Buttonbush Trail, near Salt Pond Visitor Center, are prepared in braille.

If you want to see what a nineteenth century cranberry bog was like, walk along the half mile trail through the now abandoned Pamet Cranberry Bog. It's across from the Environmental Education Center on North Point Road in Truro.

The park maintains three bicycle trails: the 1.6 mile Nauset Trail near Salt Pond Visitor Center, the 2 mile Head of the Meadow Trail in Truro, and the 5.25 mile Province Lands Trail. You can pick up a folder describing these trails at the visitor centers.

There are three bridle paths within the seashore and horses may be rented from nearby stables. Details are in the *Horse Trails of the Province Lands* folder available at the visitor centers.

Educational Programs In addition to ranger-led walks, there are other opportunities, both for adults and children, to expand their knowledge and enjoyment of Cape Cod. In the summer there are tours of the Captain Edward Penniman House and the Atwood-Higgins House, visits with surfmen who demonstrate equipment used to rescue shipwrecked seamen, shellfishing demonstrations, and evening programs featuring illustrated talks at visitor centers. Special events for seashore Junior Rangers are also conducted. For details, and to make reservations required for some activities, check at visitor centers.

The seashore sponsors a formal environmental program, National Environmental Education Development (NEED), for school groups. Schools conduct the week-long programs. The seashore provides the building, sleeping, and eating facilities and some of the educational materials. The seashore conducts a required workshop for the leaders. Groups come from as far away as the state of Virginia to take advantage of this opportunity. For information, write to NEED Coordinator at the seashore.

Hunting And Fishing   During specified seasons, hunting is permitted for deer, upland game, and migrating waterfowl. Pheasant hunting near the Marconi site is a popular activity. The Massachusetts Division of Fisheries and Wildlife and the seashore jointly manage hunting activities and hunters must abide by the rules and regulations of both. Details can be obtained by writing to the seashore Superintendent.

Fishing in the surf is a popular sport at the seashore. No license is required for salt water fishing. A state license is needed for fresh water fishing. The towns regulate shellfishing.

Oversand Vehicles (ORVs)   One of the most difficult issues the seashore has faced in recent years relates to the use of four wheel drive vehicles—often referred to as oversand or off-road vehicles or dune buggies—on the shores of the Great Beach. Before there was a national seashore, fishermen were accustomed to driving such vehicles on the sand to reach their favorite spots and residents had driven through the dunes to reach their shore-front cottages.

When large numbers of visitors came to the Cape following the seashore's establishment, conflicts developed among people who came to the shore for different reasons. Persons especially concerned about damage to the seashore's natural characteristics wanted the oversand vehicles banned or at least severely restricted. A lawsuit was filed in 1981 and tighter regulations were imposed. In September 1985, the seashore designated a restricted corridor through the dunes and along the beach in the vicinity of Provincetown as the only route open to general ORV travel. Special regulations also apply to private property owners using ORVs to travel to and from their cottages and commercial operators who conduct tours in four-wheel drive carryalls. Permits, for which there is a fee, are required for all ORVs driven on the beach. For a copy of the rules and regulations that apply, write to the Superintendent of the seashore.

Pets Pets are prohibited on nature trails and protected beaches, in public buildings, and in places that are posted. When taken to other areas, they must be under physical restraint at all times.

Birdlife On Cape Cod Look closely at Cape Cod National Seashore's logo on publications and signs and you will see a sand dune, beach grass, the sea, and a tern, a graceful seabird that finds its food in the ocean, bay, and marshes of Cape Cod. In the summer, terns (Least and Common) nest on the beach. Once nearly hunted to extinction, terns are now protected and during the nesting season you will find signs on the beach warning visitors away from nesting areas.

Cape Cod draws bird-watchers during all seasons. Over 380 species and subspecies of birds frequent the fields, waters, woods, and shore. Bookstores at the visitor centers sell a checklist of the Cape's birds showing the season and frequency. Among the rare birds watchers sometimes spot are piping plovers and peregrine falcons.

Historical/Cultural Resources A number of historical structures and sites have been placed on the National Register of Historic Places. They include the Captain Edward Penniman House and barn, the

Atwood-Higgins House, the Old Harbor Life-Saving Station, the Marconi Wireless Station site, and the site of the Great Island Tavern which nearly 250 years ago offered food and drink to shore whalers and sailors waiting to go to sea. Sites among the dunes and along Nauset Marsh known to have been frequented by Native Americans are the object of ongoing archeological research.

Cape Cod—What Of The Future?

Over four and one-half million people visit Cape Cod National Seashore every year. Though in the summer 60 percent come from the nearby region extending from Boston to Providence, Rhode Island, the seashore regularly attracts shore lovers from New York City, Chicago, Cleveland, Philadelphia, Washington, D.C., and Montreal, Canada.

How long will there continue to be a precious seashore at Cape Cod for millions of vacation-hungry Americans to visit? The seashore management recognizes that the forces of nature in the form of marine erosion are wearing the Cape away at the rate of three feet a year, more in some places than at others. They also know the futility of attempting to strike back at the sea.

But when man is responsible for the destruction of the seashore's natural resources, such as in the denuding of trees, shrubs, and grasses that hold the sands, it's a different story. Here is an illustration. Sands exposed by loss of vegetation on the high dunes in the Province Lands migrated across the main road to Provincetown, and threatened to fill up Pilgrim Lake. In 1985 the seashore mounted a massive effort in which a contractor, seashore staff, and 487 concerned volunteers replanted fifty-six acres of dunes in an attempt to stabilize the fragile landscape.

If all those who enjoy Cape Cod's fragile beauty and superb recreational opportunities share this same concern and use the seashore's resources wisely, massive efforts of this sort may never again be necessary and Cape Cod will endure long enough for many generations of future Americans to enjoy.

For more information, contact:

Superintendent
Cape Cod National Seashore
South Wellfleet, MA 02663
Phone: 508/349–3785

Cape Cod Chamber of Commerce
Junction Routes 6 and 132
Hyannis, MA 02601
Phone: 508/362–3225

Park Supervisor
Roland E. Nickerson State Park
Brewster, MA 02631
Phone: 508/896–3491

Fire Island National Seashore

There's Fire On The Island Tonight

W as it the great fires burning on the island night and day under whaler's cauldrons that gave rise to the name? Or was it a series of cartographer's errors in misreading a Dutch mapmaker's notation of "vier" as "fier," then "fire," or the reference to "five" islands near the western inlet to Great South Bay? Or perhaps the impression made on the mainlanders by fires lit for nefarious purposes during the mysterious days of shipwrecks and scavengers?

No one is certain but Fire Island seems aptly named, though today the word more properly refers to the burning passion for the island held by thousands of its devotees.

Fire Island lies within the most densely populated region of the United States, centered around New York City. Pressures of urban and suburban living require outdoor recreational outlets for pent-up energies and weary spirits. In the midst of heated battles over proposed ways to fill a perceived need, one solution won out and Congress stopped the clock on Fire Island. The results were:

- A 20 mile stretch of barrier island plus several bay islands saved from further development;

- The ground laid for the designation of seven miles of the island as a federal wilderness area, the only one in New York State;

- A commitment made to seventeen island communities that the federal government would cooperate with local governing authorities in retaining their chosen cultural patterns;

- Long stretches of ocean beach and a rare "sunken" maritime forest saved for the enjoyment of all Americans, not just those who reside in a certain place or who can afford to summer on the island.

Fire Island, a fragile streak of sand 32 miles long, is one of several barrier islands south of New York State's Long Island that bear the brunt of the Atlantic Ocean's storm-driven assaults before they strike the "mainland." Great South Bay, haven for fishermen and recreational boaters, lies between Fire Island and Long Island.

Like Cape Cod, Long Island's and Fire Island's origins are in glacial action occurring many thousands of years ago. When the glaciers, or ice sheets, moved southward, they stopped just short of the present location of Fire Island. Glacial streams fanned out, carrying rocks, silt, and sand over the coastal plains. In some places the debris piled up, forming high ridges on the landscape. The ocean was far lower than it is today. When the ice sheets melted, the seas rose. In the process the river valley that is Long Island Sound was deepened and the nearby ridges became Long Island.

In time, the sea gnawed away at the eastern end of Long Island and longshore currents pushed sand from the tip at Montauk and from Southampton westward, creating a narrow sandspit. Ocean winds and waves brought more sand to the spit, making it higher and wider. Fire Island became a separate entity when the spit was breached at

Moriches Inlet to the east and at Fire Island Inlet on the west.

The shaping and reshaping of Fire Island by natural forces is a never-ending process, one that often draws lots of public attention. Dramatic evidence of the continuing accretion of the island's western tip can be seen at Fire Island Lighthouse. Originally built near the island's western edge, the lighthouse is now nearly five miles from Fire Island Inlet.

The island has an eleven percent chance of being hit by a major tropical storm or hurricane every year. Storms coming from the northeast have caused significant damage on the average of every 1.2 years. Ever since 1938 when an unexpected hurricane devastated the island, news of approaching hurricanes and nor'easters has been widely circulated. Controversies over proposed regulations affecting the rebuilding of storm-battered houses located within a shifting Dune District are featured news stories.

The island is so narrow, no more than one-half mile at its widest point, and so popular that conservationists, home owners, sportsmen, and government authorities alike agree that only by careful regulation and cooperation can its precious resources continue to be a source of enjoyment for Americans and a benefit to the nation.

Fire Island National Seashore is an anomaly. Within its boundaries are seventeen "exempt" communities,[1] some with as few as forty houses, that run the social gamut from traditional to late twentieth century lifestyles. Some communities, inhabited by third and fourth, even fifth, generation Fire Island vacationers, diligently preserve the traditions of their founders. Some, more recently developed, are oriented to the sports and recreational in-

[1] The 1964 legislation provided that property within these communities would not be subject to condemnation so long as it is used in accordance with local zoning regulations approved by the Secretary of the Interior.

terests of suburban families with young and teenage children. A few are gathering places for singles and "groupers" seeking active adult sports and all-night parties. Fire Island's notoriety perhaps stems from the flamboyance of many artistically talented New Yorkers who have extolled the virtues of Fire Island in books, plays, and media interviews.

All communities passionately defend their lifestyles from intrusion. The communities, mostly on the western end of the island, were there before the national seashore. The seashore has filled in the island spaces between and around them and other non-federally-owned areas, notably the parks that were established on the island by various local governments before 1964.

Homes on Fire Island, like national seashore beaches, are not easy to get to. You have to go by ferry or leave your car in a lot at either end of the island and wend your way to your destination. There is no road on the island on which conventional cars may travel, and only a limited group of people are permitted to drive oversand vehicles on the island's center strip between the dunes, designated the Burma Road, or on the beach.

A few hundred hardy souls live on the island year-round, but in summer people flock there from city and suburbs and the population swells to more than 20,000, not counting those who come only for the day.

Fire Island Before The National Seashore

Before an enterprising innkeeper first envisioned Fire Island's resort possibilities and built the Surf Hotel on the western end in 1857, few people were bold enough to spend a night on the island. Only the brave and the self-reliant ventured to the island and they did so for economic reasons.

Seventeenth century colonists, having learned the rudiments of shore whaling from Indians, sharpened their whaling skills and soon a whaling industry thrived on Long Island, encompassing parts of Fire Island. By 1750, however, whalers had to roam far out to sea in search of their prey and shore whaling ceased. Only a notation on a map of seashore property designating Whalehouse Point, once the site of a whaling station, recalls the days of harpoons, look-outs, whale boats, and try-works on Fire Island.

Other early Long Island settlers boated across the bay to collect salt marsh hay for mulching, thatch, and fodder, to catch horseshoe crabs, or to take cattle to graze there.

Fire Island's remoteness attracted entrepreneurs of another sort. It's believed that at one time enclosures were built on the island to hold slaves in transit. Pirates are known to have buried treasure there. One man is reputed to have built fires to lure ships to their doom on off-shore sandbars and then scavenge the cargo that floated to shore. In modern times, the island gained fame during Prohibition days. Its off-shore waters served as a rendezvous for transferring great quantities of outlawed liquor from ocean-going vessels to coast-wise rum-runners for which the New York City market seemed limitless.

While much of Fire Island's history involves people taking advantage of its location and its resources for personal gain, some islanders devoted their energies to serving the needs of others. The keepers of the lighthouse and the members of the U.S. Life-Saving Service are remembered and honored in national seashore programs and exhibits.

By the early 1800s, it was clear to the leaders of the young nation, largely dependent on the sea for increasing their supply of goods and population, that there should be more lighthouses to aid transatlantic and coastal shipping. By then New York City was a major seaport and many ship captains were unfamiliar with the coastal barrier islands and sandbars they had to pass on their way to the city. A light-house at Montauk Point on the eastern tip of Long Island had been aiding coastal navigation since 1797 but pressure built up for another lighthouse further along the shore. Finally, the first Fire Island Lighthouse, built on the western edge of the island, went into operation in 1826.

Wrecks continued, however, and in 1858, another, higher structure was built close to the old one which was torn down. The new lighthouse was equipped with the most up-to-date Fresnel lens and its signal was visible 23 miles out to sea. After over a century of service, its light was extinguished on December 31, 1973 and an automated strobe light on a nearby water tower replaced it as a navigational aid.

There's something about a lighthouse that draws an emotional response. Perhaps because the lighthouse is a symbol of man's efforts to help those searching a way through the darkness. Or maybe it is its historical significance. Or possibly there is a sadness at the sight of an object, once a thing of beauty, fallen into a state of deterioration. Fire Island Lighthouse was scheduled to be demolished in 1981, but, like others along the coasts of the U.S., the lighthouse had its defenders. A group of private citizens banded together as the Fire Island Lighthouse Preservation Society and launched a massive fund-raising effort. An outpouring of support from all segments of society made it possible to fund the restoration of the lighthouse and the keeper's quarters and convince Congress to appropriate money for site restoration. The light was relit on May 25, 1986 and a visitor center was opened in the adjacent keeper's quarters.

Until Congress established the Revenue Marine Bureau in 1871, and its successor, the U.S. Life-Saving Service in 1878, most of the rescue efforts off the shores of Fire Island were performed by volunteers. The federal government built huts at intervals along the shore and stocked them with lifesaving equipment (lifeboats, hawsers, and lanterns, among other items) and emergency provisions (e.g., stoves, tea kettles, cast iron pots, firewood, matches, drinking water) for shipwreck survivors. The exploits of many heroic Long Island volunteers have gone down in the annals of rescue attempts.

Finally the federal government set up official Life-Saving Stations, seven of them on the beaches of present-day Fire Island, and manned them with paid surfmen obligated to follow a strict routine of patrol and rescue drill. By the time the Life-Saving Service was merged into the U.S. Coast Guard in 1915, the men of the Life-Saving Service had saved the lives of thousands of people on both bay and ocean sides of the island and salvaged ships and cargo worth millions of dollars.

Fire Island began to emerge as a recreational center in the mid 1800s. Long Islanders and city dwellers discovered the pleasures of boating, swimming, and fishing in the bay and in the ocean. They picnicked or ate at the chowder houses, pavilions, and inns that began to appear on the island. The Surf Hotel's owner lured guests to his elegant resort by facilitating transportation from the Long Island railroad across the bay to the beach and advertising that "every person who has ever visited this place suffering from the effects of fever and ague has, in every instance, been restored to health."

The Surf Hotel's good days unexpectedly came to an end in the fall of 1892. Cholera broke out on a boat returning from Europe where an epidemic was raging and the state of New York chose to house the quarantined passengers at the Surf Hotel which was closed for the season. The hotel never recovered from this episode.

The Making Of The Fire Island National Seashore

Other vacation-centered communities, each with a distinct character, began to spring up on the island around the turn of the century and after World Wars I and II. By the 1960s Fire Island's sunshine, beaches, and fun-loving atmosphere were so famous that people became concerned about the future of the island. They began to debate the merits of alternative actions that would affect its development.

The most controversial proposal was vigorously pushed for nearly forty years by its powerful author, Robert Moses, master park and road builder, who served both as New York State Commissioner of Parks and head of the Long Island State Park Commission. He wanted to build a four lane concrete road down the center of the island. The road, he said, would "anchor" the island, saving it from ocean assaults. Furthermore, it would make the whole island easily accessible to New York City's throngs.

Time and time again Fire Island property owners, supported by conservationists and newspapers, mobilized to oppose the road. They knew it would alter the ambience of the island. Equally important, it would have destroyed vast areas of undeveloped natural beauty which had been cited as particularly valuable to the nation in *Our Vanishing Shoreline,* a report issued in 1956 following a federal survey of the Atlantic and Gulf coastlines.

There were some close calls. Moses gained the support of many state and local officials and real estate interests, but never enough to overcome all the governmental hurdles. By the time Moses, past seventy years of age, relinquished his official park and road-building responsibilities to head the New York World's Fair Commission in the early

1960s, a move to create a national seashore on Fire Island was well under way. The law establishing the seashore was signed by President Lyndon B. Johnson on September 11, 1964.

Fire Island National Seashore Today

In establishing Fire Island National Seashore, Congress set out to preserve certain "relatively unspoiled and undeveloped beaches, dunes and other natural features" that were valued as "unspoiled areas of great natural beauty in close proximity to large concentrations of urban population." That is the great distinction of Fire Island National Seashore. Millions of people can escape the pressures of urban living and lie on the sundrenched beaches of Fire Island, swim in mild ocean waters, scan the horizon for passing ships, and walk quiet trails from ocean to bay and through a maritime forest all in a one day's outing. Fire Island is only 50 miles from downtown Manhattan and less than that from all parts of Long Island.

An excursion to Fire Island is mostly a summertime event. During this season, ferries to the seashore's beaches and to the communities run very frequently and the parking lots at the state and county parks at both ends of the island fill up rapidly on weekends.

The island does have its spring and fall visitors—beach lovers who enjoy a brisk walk along the shore in relative isolation. Fall is the time to view migrating waterfowl in bay waters, fish in the surf, and watch Monarch butterflies feeding on milkweed as they store up energy for the long flight to Mexico.

Only the robust respond to the urge to walk the beach in winter. Harsh winter weather changes the beach. No longer is it wide and gently sloping to the water's edge. Winds blowing from the north push the sand back into the ocean, flattening and narrowing the beach and building up the sandbar off-shore. Great South Bay sometimes ices over in the coldest winter months. When the weather begins to moderate, big chunks of ice pile up on Fire Island's bayside. This is the time when the island is quiet, There are few human visitors, and white-tailed deer, fox, rabbits, and other animals rarely seen in summer, roam freely.

How To Get There

If you don't come from New York City or Long Island, you must become familiar with Long Island's major west to east highways that roughly parallel Fire Island. Depending on where your trip originates, you will probably use either the Long Island Expressway or the Southern State Parkway. You can take roads south from either of these highways to whichever seashore facility you plan to visit. Be prepared for your travel to take longer than you might think—allow 1 1/2 to 2 hours from New York City, because congestion and road repair often impede your travel.

If you plan to go to the lighthouse area, take the Sagtikos State Parkway from the Long Island Expressway to the Robert Moses Causeway. From the Southern State Parkway, take Exit 40. The Causeway crosses Captree Island to Robert Moses State Park on Fire Island. Turn left and drive to Parking Field #5.

To reach the ferry terminal for the trip to Sailors Haven take Veterans Highway (State Route 454) from the Long Island Expressway, then right on Lakeland Avenue, crossing Sunrise Highway, to Sayville. Follow the signs to the terminal. From the Southern State Parkway, take Exit 44 to Sunrise Highway, then Lakeland to Sayville.

For the ferry to Watch Hill, take the Patchogue-Holbrook Road from any of the major west to east highways. In Patchogue, signs will direct you to the Fire Island National Seashore Ferry Terminal.

To go to Smith Point West take the William Floyd Parkway from the west-east highways, crossing Narrow Bay to Smith Point County Park where you can park while visiting the seashore.

Where To Stay

Private Accommodations The best place to stay is with a friend or relative who lives on Long Island. Hotels and motels on Long Island are expensive. If that isn't possible, information about hotels in Fire Island communities or motels located on the mainland with easy access to ferries to Fire Island can be obtained from The Long Island Tourism and Convention Commission.

Camping Fire Island's only park-maintained campsites are at Watch Hill. Reservations for the twenty-five sites offered from mid-May to mid-October are made through a lottery system. An application to participate in the lottery may be obtained in January of each year by sending a legal-sized self-addressed stamped envelope to Fire Island National Seashore, 120 Laurel Street, Patchogue, NY 11772. Starting May 1, telephone reservations for sites not yet reserved may be made by calling 516/597–6633. There is no fee and stays are limited to a maximum of five days and four nights.

The seashore also permits primitive camping at four sites in the wilderness area. State parks on Long Island at East Islip and at Wading River have facilities for camping, including trailers. Reservations are required.

What To Do At Fire Island

The Beaches If the sun is out, Fire Island's beaches, running east to west, have day-long sunshine. And sunshine, mild summertime temperatures, and fine white sandy beaches gently sloping to the ocean are a combination that's hard to beat either for relaxation or for

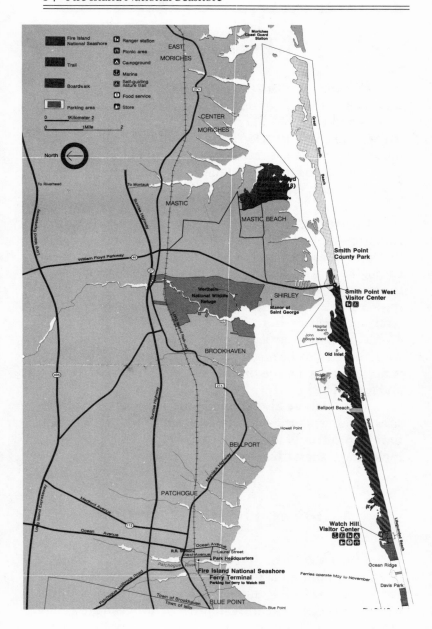

Continued on next page

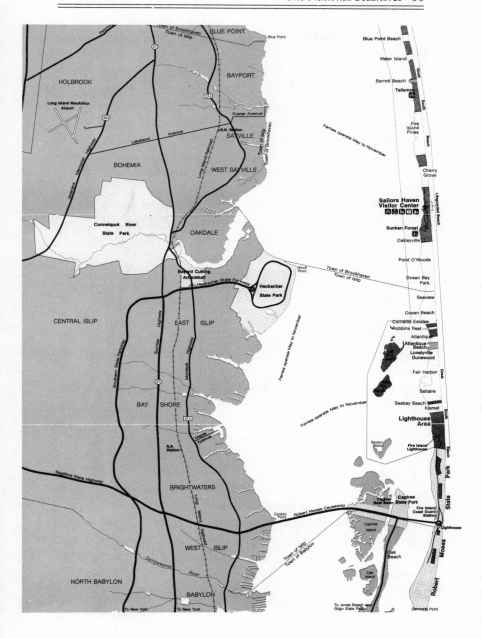

stretching out body kinks induced by a tension-filled work-week.

The national seashore's beach extends from Smith Point West which borders Suffolk County's Smith Point County Park, to the Fire Island Lighthouse area, bordering Robert Moses State Park. Most of the seashore's activities take place at four major sites: Smith Point West, Watch Hill, Sailors Haven, and the Lighthouse. There are visitor centers with interpretive displays and publications for sale at each of these places.

The Smith Point West Visitor Center is open year-round. Walks, talks and special events are conducted daily in the summer. For detailed information, call 516/281–3010.

Watch Hill offers a variety of activities. The beach is lifeguarded from late June to Labor Day. Picnic tables, solar-heated showers, and restrooms are available from May to mid-October. A concessionaire operates a 150 slip marina from mid-May to mid-October. A snack bar, restaurant, and small grocery are open during the busiest periods. It is the site of the seashore's only campground (reservations required). The visitor center is open only from the end of June until Labor Day. For specific information, call 516/597–6455.

To reach Watch Hill, take the ferry, a 25 minute trip, from the national seashore terminal in Patchogue. Parking is free at the terminal.

The beach at Sailors Haven is lifeguarded from late June to Labor Day. There is a small concession with a snack bar and souvenirs, groceries, and ice for sale. There are also picnic tables, cold showers, and restrooms. In summer, seashore rangers conduct a number of programs, demonstrations, and guided walks for both children and adults. The visitor center is open during specified times from spring until fall. To check on exact times, call 516/597–6183.

To get to Sailors Haven, take the ferry from Browns River in Sayville, a 30 minute trip. There is a charge for parking at private parking lots near the ferry dock.

Surfing And SCUBA Diving Surfing is permitted along the seashore's beaches except at lifeguarded beaches, marinas, and marked channels. However the sandbars on which the waves break are close to the beach and rides are short. SCUBA diving around shipwrecks a few miles off shore appeals to experienced sports divers.

The Trails The winding trail through Fire Island's rare sunken forest near Sailors Haven is the most unusual of the seashore's several nature trails. A visitor to Sailors Haven would surely have missed a fascinating experience if he did not walk the clearly-marked boardwalk through this dark woodland oasis naturally formed in the depression between the dunes of a sunwashed barrier island. The entire length of the sunken forest is accessible to the handicapped.

Credit for saving the sunken forest goes to a group of nature-loving citizens who, in the late 1950s, became alarmed at the news that this unique maritime forest was on the verge of development. They formed an organization and purchased the tract with the intention of maintaining it as a nature preserve or donating it to a government entity that would do the same.

American holly trees, sassafras, red cedar, and shadblow thrive in this primeval forest. The marshy floor supports ferns, wild sarsaparilla, and mayflowers and provides home and food to raccoons and other mammals. Wind-driven salt spray has sheared off the tops of the trees, forming a protective canopy, cooling the path even on the warmest days.

A nature trail near the Smith Point West Visitor Center is accessible to the handicapped. At all of the visitor centers, you can obtain interpretive brochures explaining the sites and natural surroundings along the short, easily traversed trails from ocean-facing dunes to the bay at these locations.

In 1980 Congress designated a seven mile length of the island running west from the Smith Point facility as a Wilderness Area. Except for a 17-acre ocean to bay strip in the middle, owned by the village of Bellport, by the early 1990s this entire section of the island will appear to be in a primeval state when the few remaining structures will be removed. Even now the area offers the dedicated hiker a chance to walk in solitude in the peak summer season as well as at other times.

The Fire Island Lighthouse In the summer of 1986, Fire Island's lighthouse area became a major seashore attraction. The first floor of the keeper's quarters, restored by privately-raised funds, was opened to the public as a museum depicting significant events in Fire Island's history. It also serves as a visitor center where seashore visitors can get information, purchase publications and souvenirs, and obtain a free printed guide for the Lighthouse Trail.

It is expected that restoration of the exterior of the lighthouse will be completed by the 1988 season and the black and white striped tower will once more serve as an inspiring landmark for persons on land, bay, and sea. The lighthouse is listed on the National Register of Historic Places.

To reach the lighthouse area, take the Robert Moses Causeway to the Robert Moses State Park and park at State Parking Field #5. From there, walk a short distance to the beginning of the .6 mile boardwalked trail to the visitor center. Parking for cars with disabled persons parking stickers is provided on seashore property close to the lighthouse. For further information, call 516/661–2556.

The William Floyd Estate Fire Island National Seashore includes one National Park Service unit that is on the Long Island mainland. In 1976 a lovely historic old home and surrounding property overlooking Moriches Bay, was donated to the National Park Service by one of the descendants of the original builder and it became the responsibility of the Superintendent of Fire Island National Seashore to administer it.

The oldest part of the house was built in 1724 by Nicoll Floyd. Succeeding generations farmed and later vacationed there. Members of the family served in local, state, and federal positions but the most well-known, for whom the estate is named, was William Floyd. He signed the Declaration of Independence, served in the New York Senate and was elected to the first U.S. House of Representatives.

The property now includes a twenty-five room house, eleven outbuildings, and 613 acres of forest, field, and marsh. It is open to visitors Wednesday through Sunday from April 1 to October 31. Volunteers provide a free guided tour of the house. A pamphlet is offered to those who wish to take a self-guided tour of the grounds which are landscaped and maintained in the traditional patterns of former owners.

The estate is located in Mastic Beach. To reach the grounds, take the William Floyd Parkway from Mastic south to Havenwood Drive. At Havenwood, take a left turn and follow signs to the estate. For further information, call 516/399–2030.

Hunting And Fishing Fire Island's bay and ocean waters are popular with fishermen year-round, but especially in the fall. Bluefish and flounder are sought in the bay and fishermen surfcast in the ocean for bluefish, mackerel, and weakfish (sea trout).

Fishing is permitted everywhere on federal land except in heavy use areas such as swimming beaches and marinas. No license is required.

Waterfowl hunting is the only type of hunting permitted. State regulations apply.

Oversand Vehicles (ORVs) Four-wheel drive vehicles are permitted on the mid-island path, the Burma Road, and on the beach but there are many restrictions. Environmentalists and other seashore users want ORV travel severely reduced. The issue is complicated. The only way people who live on the island can get around or be serviced by utilities and other essential public services is by the use of four-wheel drive vehicles.

The controversy therefore primarily relates to the use of ORVs for recreational purposes. Permits are required and only a limited number of them are available. Vehicles may be driven only at the east end of the seashore during specified times. They are not allowed on the beach during the summer.

A series of proposals and counter-proposals on how to regulate ORV travel has been offered in recent years. In regulating vehicular traffic, it is the intention of the seashore to protect the seashore's resources while at the same time living up to its promise not to jeopardize the servicing of the existing communities. For information on current regulations and applications for ORV driving permits, contact the Smith Point West Visitor Center by calling 516/281–3010.

Pets Pets are permitted on Fire Island so long as they are leashed. A small fee is charged for taking them on ferries. Pets are not allowed on swimming beaches or at the William Floyd Estate.

Fire Island—A Local Treasure

When Congress authorized the establishment of Fire Island National Seashore, it was clear that it intended to save some of the nation's treasured coastal resources and make them accessible to people living in the confining circumstances of a big city and its bursting suburbs. And it has turned out that way. Only seven percent of the seashore's visitors come from outside the greater New York metropolitan area.

It's not surprising that few people who live much beyond the borders of New York City set out to spend a week's vacation at Fire Island National Seashore. However Fire Island *is* a *national* seashore and it offers to all people the same beautiful beaches, nature trails, and glimpse of maritime history that New Yorkers enjoy.

For More Information, Contact:

Superintendent
Fire Island National Seashore
120 Laurel St.
Patchogue, NY 11772
Phone: 516/289–4810

Ferries to Sailors Haven from Sayville
516/589–8980

Ferries to Watch Hill from Patchogue
516/597–6455 or 516/475–1665

Long Island Tourism and Convention Commission
Nassau Coliseum
Uniondale, NY 11553
Phone: 516/794–4222

Park Manager
Heckscher State Park
East Islip, NY 11730
Phone: 516/581–2100

Park Manager
Wildwood State Park
Wading River, NY 11792
Phone: 516/929–4262

Assateague Island National Seashore

"Three creeks lying 100 paces or more north of the second inlet above Chincoteague Island.... At the head of the third creek to the northward is a bluff facing the Atlantic Ocean with three cedar trees... each about 1⅓ yards apart. Between the trees I buried in ten iron bound chests bars of silver, gold, diamonds and jewels...."

I t is no wonder pirate Captain Charles Wilson's brother never found the booty. Captain Wilson wrote these directions for him while awaiting hanging in a London prison in 1750. The Atlantic Ocean, master of Assateague Island, then and now, changes the configuration of the island at will, and the natural features seen on one day may be markedly different on the next.

Wilson's treasure may still lie deep within the sands of Assateague Island—on shore or off shore. No record exists that indicates anyone has found it. It may never be found unless the ocean yields a clue.

Assateague Island is a lengthy strip of sand which has more or less been in its present configuration along the coast of Maryland and Virginia for about 4,000 years. It never was and is not now of a fixed dimension. During its history it has been several islands and it has been a portion of a peninsula extending northward into Delaware. Navigable inlets have been created by storm-induced waves, and then in a few days, a few months, sometimes 10 or 20 years later, filled in—at least eleven times in the last few hundred years.

The angle of the waves hitting the beaches of Assateague is such that sand, and therefore the island, is constantly pushed south and west. Trunks of pine trees, once forming forests on the island's interior, have later shown up at the ocean's edge.

There is no permanence to sands, vegetation, or structures on Assateague. Dynamism is the name of the game.

Though the search for gold, silver, and jewelry is not what lures the beachgoer to Assateague Island National Seashore today, there *are* treasures. Treasures of the spirit. For the person who rejoices in a solitary walk on the beach, the discovery of a sea-washed perfect shell, a quiet walk through a maritime wood, a glimpse of a legendary shaggy pony living in the wild, untamed and unfed by man, Assateague Island National Seashore has much to offer. And it's all within a few hours' drive of thirty million people.

Assateague Before The National Seashore

Assateague Island, named for one of the bands of coastal Indians who sometimes visited the island for the rich seafood harvest opportunities, never was heavily populated. The earliest colonial inhabitants were a handful of men employed by mainland-based gentry to watch over cattle and horses grazing on open range.

Most of the small number of hardy souls who settled on Assateague Island did so to make a living from the sea. For about a hundred years, ending in the mid-nineteenth century, men extracted salt from the ocean for use in food preservation. Others supported families by fishing for oysters and crabs and catching menhaden for processing into oil and fertilizer.

Salvaging cargoes from shipwrecks—sugar, molasses, meat, lumber, and other products important to early Americans—was an early—though illegal—source of income. In 1782 the state of Virginia tried to stop the looting. An Office of Commissioner of Wrecks was set up to lead efforts to salvage goods for the benefit of their rightful owners. In 1799, under pressure from its neighbor, Maryland also appointed a wreck-master.

By 1833, a lighthouse keeper was manning the first Assateague lighthouse provided by Congress in recognition of the importance of minimizing losses to the young nation's growing commercial sailing fleet.

From 1875 to 1915, a valiant few operated four lifesaving stations set up at key points to provide additional help to ships in trouble off the coast and rescue stranded seamen.

Perhaps the first attempt to attract outsiders to the island as visiting vacationers came with the establishment of Scott's Ocean House, on the bay side of the island near Green Run Inlet, the site of one of the island's small communities. For nearly 25 years in the late nineteenth century, guests came by stagecoach and boat from Wilmington, Baltimore, Washington, and other mid-coast cities to relax and enjoy the sun, water, and sea breezes.

But time passed the inn by. Ocean City, Maryland became the "in" coastal resort of the area, largely because it was easier to get to. In the early 1900s Assateague Island, once again became a "quiet" place, an isolated island, the destinies of its few residents inextricably linked with maritime forces.

In 1915 the Life-Saving Service gave way to the U.S. Coast Guard, by then better equipped to take over the function of coastal rescue. The second Assateague lighthouse (built in 1867 to be taller and more powerful than the first one), fueled initially by whale oil, then kerosene, became electrified in 1932. Residents tired of the constant struggle to save their homes from the destruction of hurricanes and nor'easters; some found their livelihood threatened when a private landowner cut off their access to the sea. Seeking better jobs, people began moving homes and possessions to more stable communities.

Two great storms in the space of 30 years reshaped Assateague Island—from the ocean to the bay and from the north to the south. How people responded to these events illustrates the constant tug of war between man and the sea.

In 1933 a violent hurricane blasted an inlet through the peninsula in the location of what is now the northern end of Assateague Island and the southern end of Ocean City. In time, the sea undoubtedly would have closed the inlet, but the economic interests of Ocean City convinced the U.S. Army Corps of Engineers and other state and federal government officials to keep the inlet open. Jetties were built and have been maintained ever since, and necessary dredging has been done to give boats moored in the bay west of Ocean City easy access to the ocean. Large sums continue to be spent to thwart the natural processes of the sea at the north end of Assateague Island. The normal southerly drifting of sand along the shore of islands of this portion of the Atlantic has been interrupted by the jetties and Assateague's northern tip has eroded more than 1750 feet in the 50 years since the jetties were built. Oceanographers say it is sand-starved.

No longer connected to its northern neighbor, Assateague has become a truly isolated island. Some 37 miles long, it varies in width from less than one-quarter mile at its northern tip to two and one-half miles of marsh and woodland just before it hooks around Toms Cove at the sand-blown southern end. The island lies within two states—the northern 22 miles in Maryland, the southern 15 miles in Virginia.

When the National Park Service conducted its first survey of lands along the Atlantic and Gulf coasts to identify potential sites for federally owned national seaside recreation areas, Assateague did not go unnoticed. Its undeveloped status, its many natural attractions, and its nearness to urban populations qualified it as one of twelve outstanding areas recommended for eventual acquisition in a report made to the Secretary of the Interior on January 2, 1935.

The Making Of The Assateague Island National Seashore

Over the next 16 years the National Park Service kept recommending Assateague Island as a national public recreation site, and legislation was repeatedly introduced in Congress for this purpose.

A federal foothold was gained in 1943 when the Bureau of Sports Fisheries and Wildlife (now the Fish and Wildlife Service) succeeded in establishing the Chincoteague National Wildlife Refuge on the Virginia portion of the island. Funds received from the sale of Migratory Bird Hunting and Conservation Stamps ("duck stamps") were used to buy the land. The original purpose of the refuge was to support the migration of the greater snow goose. Today it provides a resting and feeding ground for over 275 species of birds.

The year 1950 brought developers into the picture. A 15-mile ocean front site in the center of the island was acquired, a road, "Baltimore Boulevard," was paved, land was subdivided and a major sales campaign was initiated to entice both vacationers and speculators to purchase. By the early 1960s, 5,850 lots had been sold.

A similar venture was undertaken at the northern end of Assateague in the mid 1950s but without much success. In time, noting the interest of the state of Maryland in acquiring land on the island for a state park, the developer of "North Ocean Beach" donated its interests in 540 island acres to the state, whereupon the Maryland General Assembly established Assateague State Park and authorized construction of a bridge to the park in 1961.

A year later, March 6, 1962, a devastating storm brought everything to a halt. Protective dunes were severed by the waves, most island structures were destroyed, and the road was largely washed out or buried. The discouraging outlook for private development on Assateague Island due to the storm rekindled interest in the island as a potential national seashore.

As luck would have it, a new federally sponsored study just two months earlier had again pointed out the need for additional seashore recreation land for a mobile urban population.

After three years of negotiating to protect the interests of the state of Maryland and the Maryland and Virginia counties in which Assateague Island is located and devising a system to compensate private land interests, legislation to create Assateague Island National Seashore was finally enacted and signed into law on September 21, 1965.

Assateague Island National Seashore Today

Though there are times when nature strikes Assateague with considerable fury, they are not frequent. Normally its temperate climate draws visitors year round. The winter beach walker, the spring canoeist, the summer sunbather, the fall wildfowlwatcher—all are attracted to Assateague.

In summer, the lifeguarded beaches are heavily populated, but anyone willing to walk a few hundred yards away from the crowd can be alone on the beach. A walk through a maritime wood, a short informational guide in hand to point out the special natural attractions, awaits the curious. A controlled sand path for off-road vehicles makes it possible for the fisherman or hunter to reach the ideal spot from which to pursue his sport. Remote camping sites are available to the backpacking camper. A child can use a seashore microscope to study the bay or learn how to cast a net and haul in fish, earning a Junior Naturalist badge. The hiker and biker will find that several hours are set aside daily for their exclusive access to a wildlife trail.

How To Get There

You must decide if you want to go either to the north end of the island, in Maryland, nine miles south of populous Ocean City, or to the south end, in Virginia, across a short bridge from Chincoteague. To go to the Maryland section, take U.S. Route 50 east, then State Route 611 south. To reach the Virginia section, take north/south U.S. Route 13, then east on State Route 175, crossing Chincoteague Island to the seashore. No road runs the length of the island.

Where To Stay

Private Accommodations If your destination is the Maryland section, your best bet is to write or call the Ocean City Visitors Information Center to obtain information about hotels, motels and private campgrounds in the area. The Chincoteague Chamber of Commerce can provide information about accommodations near the Virginia Section.

Camping See information under Maryland and Virginia sections.

The Maryland Section

A visit to the Maryland section should include a first stop at the seashore visitor center on State Highway 611 on the mainland just before the Verrazano bridge that crosses Sinepuxent Bay to the island. Pick up a brochure identifying all seashore recreation areas and a special pamphlet on Assateague's famous wild ponies. Look at the exhibits depicting seashore life. Browse through a book stall and talk to the ranger on duty. In the summer be sure to check the list of ranger-conducted nature walks, evening programs, and rescue, surf fishing, clamming and crabbing demonstrations. The center is open daily from 8:30 a.m. to 5 p.m.

Fees for a visit to Assateague Island National Seashore range from $3.00 per car, entitling driver and passengers full access to the park for seven consecutive days; $1.00 for persons over 12 years old entering by other means; to $10.00 for an annual pass to Park Service-managed areas. Holders of Golden Eagle, Golden Age and Golden Access passports are exempt from these fees.

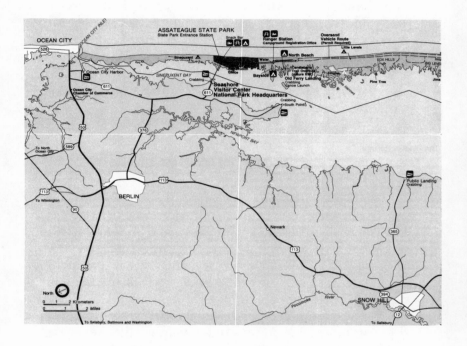

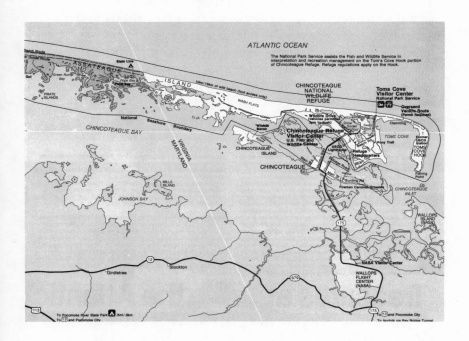

ATLANTIC OCEAN

The National Park Service assists the Fish and Wildlife Service in interpretation and recreation management on the Tom's Cove Hook portion of Chincoteague Refuge. Refuge regulations apply on the Hook.

What To Do At The Maryland Section

The Beaches There are two lifeguarded beaches. The first beach you see after crossing the bridge onto the island is Maryland's Assateague State Park. (Maryland's continued presence on the island was a condition of the legislation establishing the national seashore.) During the summer, the state park operates bath houses, a bait and tackle shop, and food service facilities. Just south of the state park is the national seashore's lifeguarded North Beach with picnic tables and a bathhouse.

Camping Assateague State Park has a modern campground with hot showers, flush toilets, and 311 spaces for campers (no electric hookups). The campground is open during spring, summer, and fall. Some campsites can be reserved for a full week during summer. For information, write to the Assateague State Park.

South of the state park, the National Park Service administers two primitive campgrounds with portable toilets and cold-water showers. One of the campgrounds is open year-round. Both individual and group campsites are available. Individual sites are on a first come, first served basis. Group sites require advance reservation. Write to the Superintendent, Assateague Island National Seashore.

Backcountry hike-in camping on the seashore beach and hike-in or canoe-in camping on the bayside is permitted at designated sites, but permits must be obtained from the seashore visitor center. The oceanside sites have a picnic table and chemical toilets. The bayside sites, located within groves of pine trees, each have a fire ring and a picnic table. Chemical toilets are provided. Oceanside camping is permitted year round. Bayside sites are open March through October. Campers must bring fresh water with them to all backcountry sites. If you go in summer, be forewarned of the occasional heavy mosquito and biting fly population and bring lots of mosquito repellent. Vacationers may use the private campgrounds on the mainland, or visit Delaware's Trap Pond State Park or Maryland's Pocomoke River State Park. Both are about a 45 minute drive inland. For a list of private campgrounds, send for *Maryland Outdoor Guide,* prepared by the Office of Tourist Development, Maryland Department of Economic and Community Development.

The Trails For a change from beach activities, take a walk on a nature trail through all the other maritime life zones. A one-mile walk on the Candleberry Trail will take you through the interdune zone, the shrub-forest zone and the marsh zone. Pick up a printed guide for your walk from a trailside box. It will identify what you are seeing and how it relates to the barrier island environment.

Either here or at other points on the seashore, depending on the season, you may see a family of Assateague Island's wild ponies. Legend has it that they are descendants of ponies shipwrecked when a Spanish galleon foundered off shore about 200 years ago. However, no research to date has been able to substantiate this romantic version of the history of the ponies. Some people think it is more likely that the ponies descended from animals taken there for free pasturage by nearby mainland settlers many years ago. If you see the ponies, heed the advice of the rangers. Look, but don't feed or touch! These animals truly are wild and people get injured from bites and kicks every year.

Canoeing You can launch a canoe into the shallow waters of Chincoteague Bay at the end of Ferry Landing Road opposite North Beach. An opportunity for quiet exploration of the salt water marshes awaits the canoe enthusiast.

Oversand Vehicles (ORVs) Oversand vehicles (ORVs) have been on Assateague Island since the late 1920s and were in widespread use when the park service took over seashore management. The use of ORVs to reach choice or lonely surf fishing areas on the beach or seashore maintained blinds for public waterfowl hunting is permitted today. To drive on the beach or specially marked trail, ORV operators must obtain a permit, for which there is a fee, have certain equipment, and abide by strict regulations. Get details by writing to the Superintendent. The ORVs-on-the-beach issue continues to be the subject of controversy.

Hunting And Fishing Hunting for wildfowl and deer is permitted as part of a broad resources management plan. Strict regulations based on state law as well as federal rules apply. Get details by writing to the Assateague Island National Seashore.

No license is required for saltwater fishing and shellfishing in designated areas.

Pets Pets are allowed in some areas in the Maryland section of the national seashore as long as they are on leashes no longer than six feet. They are *not* permitted in the seashore's lifeguard protected beach, hike-in or canoe-in campsites, Assateague State Park, or the primitive area north of the state park.

The Virginia Section

Quite a different experience awaits you on the southern end of Assateague Island. En route, you may want to stop on Chincoteague Island, which you must cross to get to the seashore. Chincoteague is rapidly transforming itself from an old, quiet fishing village into a tourist center with a variety of motels, campgrounds, restaurants, shops, and entertainment facilities.

Chincoteague gets nationwide attention on the last Wednesday and Thursday of July with the round-up and sale of Chincoteague ponies owned by the Chincoteague Volunteer Fire Department but living, by special arrangement, on the Chincoteague Wildlife Refuge, which is part of Assateague Island. On the first day of this two-day celebration, ponies rounded up by the Fire Department's "cowboys" swim across the channel from their island range to Chincoteague Island to the cheers of thousands of spectators. They are penned overnight and the foals and yearlings are auctioned off the next day. This has been a popular fund-raising event since the 1920s. Reducing the herd in this manner also helps to keep the refuge's pony population under control.

If you or the younger members of your family have read Marguerite Henry's *Misty of Chincoteague*, you will have a special feeling for both Chincoteague and the wild ponies you will see on Assateague Island.

What To Do At The Virginia Section

The Wildlife Refuge Once across the bridge onto Assateague Island, the atmosphere immediately changes. The greater part of the Virginia section is occupied by the Chincoteague National Wildlife Refuge. Though technically part of the Assateague Island National Seashore, most of the Virginia section is administered by the U.S. Fish and Wildlife Service. (The Park Service manages the recreation facilities on Toms Cove Hook.) Stop at the information center maintained by the Wildlife Refuge. It is located close to the entrance to the Wildlife Drive and well marked. It is open from 9 a.m. to 4 p.m.

every day.

The Fish and Wildlife Service collects the following entrance fees from visitors to the refuge: weekly–$3.00 per vehicle; bicyclists and walkers–$1.00; annual fee–the Federal Duck Stamp ($12.50) until July 1, 1991. Children under 16 and holders of Golden passports are not charged.

Only hikers and persons riding bicycles may traverse the 3.5 mile Wildlife Loop before 3 p.m. After 3 p.m. automobiles may drive on the road until dark.

Further along the Beach Road is an entrance to the Woodland Trail for hikers and bikers only. Whether traveling by foot or on wheels, there are great rewards on these trails for those who cherish a glimpse of wildlife in its natural habitat. Flocks of migratory birds–ducks, geese, and swans from autumn until spring, and egrets, herons, ibises, wood ducks, and other shore-birds in summer–frequent the salt marshes. You may also see deer, wild ponies, and other woodland animals.

Among the rarer species found on Assateague is one listed as endangered, the Delmarva fox squirrel, and two that are threatened, the piping plover and peregrine falcon.

For complete information on the Chincoteague National Wildlife Refuge, write the Manager, Chincoteague National Wildlife Refuge.

The Beach Follow the Beach Road to the Toms Cove Visitor's Center operated by the National Park Service. A stop at the visitor center there is highly recommended. Check out the interpretive programs being offered by the rangers and examine the artfully-done panels depicting the life zones of the barrier beach. These are enjoyable ways to learn about vegetation, bird, and animal life of each zone, from ocean to bay. Then walk the Toms Cove Nature Trail to learn about salt marshes and see an amazing number of fiddler crabs.

A variety of water-oriented recreational activities await: swimming, sunbathing, shell collecting, surf fishing, clamming, and crabbing. The beach is lifeguarded in season. Bathhouses accommodate handicapped visitors.

On busy summer weekends, you may have to wait to get to the beach. Toms Cove Hook beach is very popular and parking is especially limited since the 1984 winter storms destroyed the paved road south of the beach where 120 additional parking spaces are located. The road was rebuilt that summer, then destroyed again by another storm a few weeks later. The wisdom of constructing island parking lots in a dynamically changing area has been the subject of much controversy among conservationists, government agencies, and Chincoteague business interests and their spokesmen. It appears that the road will not be rebuilt and consideration is being given to providing alternate means for transporting people from parking areas on Chincoteague Island to the beach.

Camping There are no camping facilities in the Virginia section of the national seashore. However, a number of private campgrounds are located on Chincoteague Island. For information, write to Chincoteague Chamber of Commerce.

Pets Pets are not allowed anywhere in the Virginia section of the national seashore.

Historical/Cultural Resources Giovanni da Verrazano observed evidence of human activity when he sailed past Assateague Island in 1524, but very little evidence of the lives of the early islanders remains. The Atlantic Ocean, through overwash and other maritime assaults, has periodically reached out to claim its own. Fires of unknown origin have also caused destruction.

Two major historic structures, both in the Virginia section, do remain, however, and have been either listed or nominated for the National Register of Historic Places. They are the former Assateague Beach Coast Guard Station (nominated) on Toms Cove Hook, now owned by the National Park Service, and the 1867 lighthouse (listed), owned and operated by the Coast Guard. First built on what was then the southern tip of Assateague, wind and wave have so changed the shape of the island, that the lighthouse is now quite far inland, close to the Fish and Wildlife Service Information Center. Neither the Coast Guard Station nor the lighthouse is open to the public, but persons fascinated with the drama of lighthouse-keeping a century ago will enjoy a short walk to the base of the lighthouse and a view of its exterior.

Assateague Island: An About-face In Seashore Management

The philosophy of management of a national seashore has undergone considerable change since the mid 1960s—and no seashore offers a better example of its effect than Assateague.

Original plan for the seashore called for the building of facilities for "maximum public recreation use." There was to be a 600-acre concession area including a large restaurant, snack bar, gift shop, salt water pool, fishing piers, and a 500-unit motel. A road to traverse the entire length of the island was planned and several thousand parking spaces would be provided in four different areas.

As time to acquire land from private owners stretched out, cost figures rose and implementation of the plan was delayed. Meanwhile, a newly aroused public and the results of new scientific studies caused the plan for development to be examined in a new light. Environmental and conservation groups objected to extensive development on the barrier beach. Businesses sprouting up in Chincoteague were meeting the need for overnight accommodations and other services for seashore visitors. Most important, experience with beach erosion control at other seashores, notably Cape Hatteras, was causing questions to be raised about the wisdom of attempts to stabilize moving beaches. A new view began to take hold: that dune building and dredging of bayside estuaries destroy the natural systems that the federal government was committed to protect. By the early 1970s, new park service policies recognized that barrier islands are transient and that the building of costly and extensive permanent facilities was to be avoided. Original development plans for Assateague were dropped.

Assateague Island National Seashore today has more than two million visitors a year. It is prepared to accommodate more visitors, particularly at the Maryland section (though parking and camping can be a problem on some summer weekends). It will undoubtedly continue to be a popular destination for beachgoers from the mid-Atlantic states. As a *national* seashore, however, it is meant to be enjoyed by citizens of all states. Wherever you come from, if you love the beach and what it offers, you, too, can have a good time at Assateague Island National Seashore.

For More Information, Contact:

Superintendent
Assateague Island National Seashore
Route 2, Box 294
Berlin, MD 21811
Phone: 301/641–1441
301/641–3030 (Campground Office)

Manager
Chincoteague National Wildlife Refuge
P.O. Box 62
Chincoteague, VA 23336
Phone: 804/336–6122

Ocean City Visitors Information Center
P.O. Box 158
Ocean City, MD 21842
Attn: Public Relations Department
Phone: MD residents: 1-800-49BEACH;
residents of DE, Washington DC, NJ, PA, VA, and WVA,
and southeastern NY: 1-800-62OCEAN;
all others: 301/289–2800

Chincoteague Chamber of Commerce
P.O. Box 258
Chincoteague, VA 23336
Phone: 804/336–6161

Superintendent
Assateague State Park
Route 2, Box 293
Berlin, MD 21811
Phone: 301/641–2120

Office of Tourism Development
MD Department of Economic and Employment
Development
217 East Redwood St.
Baltimore, MD 21202
Phone: 1/800/543–1036
301/333–6611

Cape Hatteras National Seashore

"When you visit the Outer Banks, you feel you are in the domain of the sea and wind, more than of the land— and you are."

Patrick D. Crosland, *The Outer Banks*

The Outer Banks of North Carolina, of which Cape Hatteras is a significant part, embrace the most romantic group of barrier islands on the Atlantic coast. The story of these islands is one of historical firsts, mystery, piracy, tragic losses, bold rescues and man's sometimes grudging acknowledgment of the dominance of the sea.

Today Cape Hatteras National Seashore is a land of fun and sun. The fisherman casting a line into the surf off the beach at Cape Point, the surfer, swimmer, sunbather, bird-watcher, and the other nearly two million annual visitors enjoy the national seashore's beaches, marshes, breezes, and sunshine largely unmindful of the struggles of their predecessors on these long, narrow, sandy barriers.

The Outer Banks stretch more than 175 miles from the Virginia border to Shackleford Banks opposite

Beaufort,[1] protecting mainland North Carolina from the Atlantic Ocean's assault. The banks form two sides of a slightly bent diamond, stretching southeasterly from the north end to the tip of Cape Hatteras, then abruptly turning southwest to Cape Lookout Point. Just to the north of this point and starting from within the harbor formed by the spear-like backward thrust of Cape Lookout is Shackleford Banks, running eight miles east to west.

The famed Diamond Shoals, scourge of seafarers for centuries, repeat this diamond-shaped configuration in the water's depths off the coast of Cape Hatteras. Ridges of dangerous undulating sands have confounded navigators from the beginning of known coastal exploration as seamen pushed their luck to take advantage of trade winds and warm Gulf Stream waters flowing up from the tropics, passing relatively close to the shore at Cape Hatteras.

The shoals are not the only hazard. Cold ocean water streaming south from the Arctic Ocean and, at times, cold air from the mainland head out to sea to collide with warm water from the south, churning it up like a food mixer, demanding the best of men and boats to avoid disaster. Nor'easters in winter and spring, and hurricanes in summer and fall add to the challenge. The count of known shipwrecks due to weather and enemy action since the late

---

[1] This chapter applies the term "Outer Banks" to the barrier islands separated from the mainland by broad sounds, as characterized by David Stick, author of *The Outer Banks of North Carolina*.

sixteenth century—close to a thousand—indicates why this area is called the "Graveyard of the Atlantic."[2]

Geologists tell us that nowhere in the world are barrier islands so far from the mainland as at Cape Hatteras. The widest expanse of water between the seashore and the coast is Pamlico Sound—26 miles across at one point. The sounds and constantly shifting inlets are shallow.[3]

Twenty-five different inlets have remained open long enough to acquire names (sometimes the same ones in different places) and appear on printed maps. Today there are three at Cape Hatteras National Seashore: Oregon, Hatteras, and Ocracoke Inlets.

When Europeans first came to the Outer Banks, they found forests of cedar, pine, live oak, maple, hickory, and cypress trees, abundant marsh grasses that attracted waterfowl, and dense grape vines. Settlers chopped down the trees for houses, boats, and firewood and their grazing horses and cattle denuded the vegetation. It wasn't long before harsh coastal winds blew the exposed sands westward, piling them in many places into very high dunes, burying trees in their path. Many a visitor to the north end of the banks today is startled to see the swirling sands of towering Jockey's Ridge, 140 feet high, the site of a state park where hang-gliding is a popular pastime.

At other points, further south, the dunes have disappeared. The shore is flat and subject to frequent overwash. For four decades, starting in the mid 1930s, the federal government believed that the blowing sands could be halted, and put men to work building fences, planting gras-

---

[2] Even today experienced sailors warn: "If Bermuda lets you pass, then watch out for Hatteras. And if at Hatteras all is well, watch out Cape Cod don't give you hell."

[3] Openings through the island barriers are sometimes called outlets because, under certain weather conditions, the normally calm sound waters violently break through the land to the ocean.

ses, and rebuilding dunes. After spending twenty million dollars and getting only temporary results, the massive effort was abandoned.

A great body of seacoast lore revolves about Cape Hatteras. The magnificent beach at Cape Hatteras may attract you to the seashore but once there, many other fascinating experiences await you. Start with a visit to the Hatteras Island Visitor Center. Exhibits show how the "Bankers" coped with shipwrecks, harsh environment, and wars and, through it all, the need to support themselves. Excellent books and pamphlets are for sale. Many tell the tales of adventurous souls who sailed the adjacent waters and tried, some succeeding, some not, to make their fortunes from, or in spite of, this unique juxtaposition of land and coastal waters.

The Outer Banks Before The National Seashore

Cape Hatteras National Seashore occupies the better part of three of the Outer Bank islands, known today as Bodie[4] (pronounced like "body"), Hatteras and Ocracoke Islands. The islands vary in width from a few hundred feet in most parts to two miles at the widest point on Hatteras Island. The entire seashore is within the 100 year flood plain.

Not much is known about the Indians who first lived on the Outer Banks over 1500 years ago. It's believed they were Algonquins, ancestors of the Corees, Croatans, and other tribes that greeted the European explorers in the sixteenth century. They appear to have been peaceful and amply provisioned from hunting and fishing. Early European explorers found the Indians at first curious, friendly, and helpful.

Giovanni da Verrazano, an Italian sailing under French auspices, is said to be the first European to view the coast of North Carolina. In 1524 when Verrazano was searching for a short route to the Orient, his map maker noted that "one sees the Western Ocean" across an "isthmus" separating it from "this Eastern Ocean." Historians believe he was looking across the Outer Banks to Pamlico Sound.

Under Sir Walter Raleigh's leadership, the English began to explore the Outer Banks in 1584. For several months in 1585-86, a party headed by Ralph Lane fanned out from a fort built on Roanoke Island[5] to check on the surrounding countryside. The group included the artist

---

[4] Bodie, once an island, is now a sand "spit" extending southward from Virginia.

[5] Roanoke Island is between Bodie Island and the mainland.

John White whose watercolors of the flowers, animals, and Native Americans he saw are highly treasured today.

John White returned to Roanoke Island a year later to establish a permanent colony of English men, women, and children and thereby hangs an intriguing tale. The colony ran short of supplies and the Indians, who began to resent the colonists' fort building and exploring parties, became hostile. White decided to leave 116 colonists at their fort on the northern end of Roanoke Island and return to England for supplies. The party that stayed included White's daughter, Eleanor, and granddaughter, Virginia Dare, the first English child born in the New World.

Delayed because of the diversion of all English ships to fight the Spanish, when he returned to the fort in 1590, he found the settlement in ruins and no sign of the colonists. Only the word "Croatoan" carved on the palisade and "CRO" on a nearby tree gave a clue. It was assumed the colonists may have gone to live with friendly Croatan Indians. Ill-equipped for an extensive search, the expedition returned home.

To this day, nearly 400 years later, no trace of these first colonists has been found and the mystery of "the Lost Colony" has never been solved. The story is acted out each summer on the stage of Waterside Theatre, Roanoke Island, near the national seashore's administrative headquarters at Manteo.

Later English colonists from other coastal settlements were attracted to the Outer Banks because of the potential for livestock raising and commercial fishing. Sometimes shipwrecked sailors stayed. Small, isolated communities—Chicamacomico, Buxton, Kinnakeet, Hatteras, and others—were started on the sound side of the islands, protected from the ocean's fury. Left largely to themselves, the Bankers were a fiercely independent lot.

The dominant theme of records about the Outer Banks for the next 350 years is navigation and how the seafarers, islanders, and political leaders of the day determinedly coped with the attendant hazards.

The islanders were versatile. They were life-savers, volunteers at first, who incidently augmented their personal fortunes by salvaging cargo; then as proud surfmen of the U.S. Life-Saving Service.

They were tolerant of smugglers and privateers, sharing a resentment of colonial tariffs. They witnessed the short Golden Age of Piracy which ended with Blackbeard's death in a fierce hand-to-hand battle on his own ship in a cove behind the village of Ocracoke.

They were defenders of their homes from Spanish and French privateers, British raiders seeking fresh meat during the Revolution and, through a peaceful approach and a cooperative attitude, from the Union troops occupying the Confederate built forts in the early days of the Civil War.

They were self-sufficient; each man becoming a stockman, gardener, boat builder, fisherman, and hunter. Only piloting became a specialized occupation. Pilots were indispensable to both large commercial ships and naval vessels seeking passage through the Bank's narrow inlets and around dangerous shoals. They were so important to trade they were licensed and regulated by the government. At one point, they were even given land on which to build homes near the crucial inlet of Ocracoke.

Lighthouses On The Outer Banks

Up to the beginning of the nineteenth century, navigational aids were mostly confined to inlets—where men with local knowledge of shoals and shifting sands piloted ships through the inlets and the practice of lightering developed. Lightering involved unloading cargoes of heavily laden commercial vessels and storing them in warehouses for later shipment to the mainland in shallow-draft boats.

Commerce was increasing along the Atlantic coast and the waters continued to take their toll. A move to provide significant aids to coastal shipping developed.

Congress authorized the building of lighthouses. Under pressure from local interests, Shell Castle Island, just inside Ocracoke Inlet where a commercial warehousing venture was under way, was chosen as the first site. Completed in 1798, the lighthouse was more useful to ships traversing the inlet than to ships at sea. Shell Castle Island's commerce diminished with shoaling in the channel and in 1823, a lighthouse was built in the village of Ocracoke. The sparkling white stone structure, the oldest lighthouse on the North Carolina coast, still serves its purpose.

At about the same time the Shell Castle light was built, work began on a lighthouse at Cape Hatteras. It became operational in 1803. Years later, in response to complaints about its deficiencies, Congress appropriated funds for a new structure 208 feet high. It first showed its signal to ships at sea in 1870. Shortly after, it was painted in the now familiar black and white spiral bands.

The tallest and most recognized beacon in the United States, this towering structure has, over the years, faced a seemingly invincible foe—erosion. When it was built, the lighthouse was 1500 feet from the ocean. By 1935, the sea was within 100 feet. Unless something was done to halt the encroachment of the sea, the foundation would be undermined and the lighthouse would collapse.

In 1936 the U.S. Coast Guard, responsible for navigational aids, moved its warning system to a steel skeleton in Buxton Woods, a mile west, and donated the lighthouse to the National Park Service. However, in 1949 when it seemed that shoreline erosion had been stabilized, the lighthouse was reactivated and it is currently operational.

Many efforts have been made to save this national landmark. Steel groins and various types of sand barriers have been built. Even artificial sea grass was installed in the surf on the theory that an "underwater snow fence" would trap sand, causing it to build up the beach. Nothing has worked. The surf once again is closing in on the lighthouse.

A public "Save the Lighthouse" campaign attracted many supporters throughout the nation. After a lengthy period of public discussion of what to do about the lighthouse, the National Park Service has decided to build a revetment, that is a seawall of steel, concrete, and rocks, around the lighthouse. It is recognized that because of the rise in the level of the ocean, 50 to 100 years from now, the lighthouse complex may well become an island.

Three lighthouses have been built on Bodie Island just north of Oregon Inlet. The first, built in 1848, didn't last long because of poor construction; the second was destroyed by the Confederate army in 1861; the third, constructed 10 years later, extends 156 feet above sea level. The light topping the black and white circular striped tower, is visible for 19 miles.

None of the lighthouses within the national seashore are now open to the public. But a stroll down a quiet village street gives the visitor a close view of the Ocracoke lighthouse and you can walk around the Cape Hatteras and Bodie Island lighthouses when you go to the seashore visitor centers located in their former keepers' quarters.

In addition to building lighthouses, other ways were sought to help ships avoid treacherous Diamond Shoals. In 1806 after studying the possibility of building a lighthouse and permanently mooring buoys at the shoals, surveyors concluded "any building situated 15 or 20 miles in the ocean could (not) possibly withstand the continued shock of the sea, impelled by a boisterous gale for three thousand miles."

In 1824 a specially designed lightship was anchored off the edge of Diamond Shoals. A few years later it ended up on the shore, torn from its mooring in a severe storm. A "Texas tower" now marks the shoals for passing ships.

Shipwrecks And Life-Savers

"She struck about 10 o'clock at night, bilged in a few minutes, and got on her beam ends, every sea making a fair breach over her. At 12 o'clock her deck blew up and washed away altogether, and broke in two near the hatchway. The bow part turned bottom up, the stern part righted. Mr. Kinley (passenger) and Wm. Bartlett (seaman) washed off. The remainder of us got on the taffil rail, and that all under water. About 2 o'clock a.m., Mr. Campbell (the other passenger) and Wm. Shoemaker (cook) expired and dropped from the wreck. About 4 o'clock, Jesse Hand (seaman) became so chilled that he washed off. At daylight, Mr. Hawley (mate) died, and fell from along side of me into his watery grave, which I expected every moment would be my own lot. But thro' the tender mercy of God, I survived on the wreck for 24 hours alone.

"On Monday morning, about 2 o'clock, the stern broke away and I went with it. At sunrise I was taken off, so much mangled and bruised that few persons thought I could survive. I, however, am gaining, having received the kindest treatment, and every possible care from the inhabitants . . ."

This account is from a letter written by Captain Hand of the sloop *Henry,* bound from New York to Charleston, wrecked by a hurricane in December 1819, reprinted in *Graveyard of the Atlantic, Shipwrecks of the North Carolina Coast,* by David Stick.

Detailed accounts of shipwrecks began to appear in newspapers and court records with increasing frequency after the War of 1812.

In 1848 a law was passed providing for life saving stations along the east coast. By the end of the 1870s, 25 stations were in operation along the North Carolina coast, spaced about 7 miles apart. In June 1882, twelve stations were located in what is now the area of the national seashore.

The men of the U.S. Life-Saving Service followed a strict routine, patrolling the beach at night ready with their flares to warn ships of dangerous coastal waters. When necessary, they quickly fired a breeches buoy to foundering boats near enough to reach or, if beyond that, they launched boats and rowed through the pounding sea to take survivors from the water, ships and floating debris.

Stories of heroic rescues abound in the annals of the Life-Saving Service. Many, including accounts involving ships sunk by enemy action in World Wars I and II, are retold in David Stick's *Graveyard of the Atlantic* and in exhibits at seashore visitor centers. One of the most popular ranger-conducted programs at the national seashore is a recreation of a Life-Saving Service rescue drill at the Chicamacomico Coast Guard Station in Rodanthe. In summer, the National Park Service and the Chicamacomico Historical Association cooperate to show visitors what life was like for the surfmen of the Life-Saving Service.

The Life-Saving Service was combined with the Revenue Cutter Service to form the United States Coast Guard in 1915.

The Outer Banks—A New Way Of Life Emerges

The importance of the Outer Banks to commercial shipping declined after the Civil War. Hatteras Inlet, which had surpassed Ocracoke Inlet as the prime transit point from the Atlantic to the sounds following a storm in the 1840s, could no longer handle large, modern vessels. Railroads and turnpikes on the mainland and a newly built inland waterway offered more dependable methods of transport.

For a time, commercial fishing became a primary source of income. Local residents also began to find jobs working for the federal government—at lighthouses, life-saving stations, post offices, and in the construction of federal facilities.

Shortly after the turn of the century, the remoteness and almost constant windy weather was responsible for another historic "first" on the Outer Banks. Seeking a place to try out their experiments with kites, gliders, and "flying machines," Wilbur and Orville Wright contacted the U.S. Weather Bureau. Kill Devil Hills, near Kitty Hawk on the Outer Banks, offered the right combination of high sand dunes, wind velocity, and minimal population. In the fall of 1900, they began the first of numerous experiments on the steep sand hills. After three years of working to perfect their theories and equipment, on December 17, 1903, they conducted man's first successful attempt to fly a heavier-than-air machine.

On occasion during the eighteenth century, main-landers came to the Outer Banks for summer visits, seeking fresh sea air as an antidote for chills and fever attributed to the vapors of the eastern North Carolina swamps. Others came to hunt or fish. During the mid to late nineteenth century, tourism as an industry began to appear when a hotel and vacation cottages were built at Nags Head. Schooners transported people to the Outer Banks from mainland cities.

In the 1920s, tourists were coming in greater numbers and plans were made to build roads and bridges to facilitate travel. Work was begun on a national monument com-memorating the achievements of the Wright Brothers at Kill Devil Hills. Landowners subdivided property for vaca-tion homes. The Bankers were ready for a new industry.

Making The Nation's First National Seashore

Some people worried about what extensive development would do to the Outer Banks' fragile resources; and yet a boost to the economy was needed. A possible solution centered on a proposal to establish a "Coastal Park for North Carolina and the Nation" on the Outer Banks. In 1933, in a move to attract national attention to the banks' seashore delights, a major area newspaper gave prominence to the proposal.

At that time, there were no national parks on the nation's barrier beaches. The proposed park would include the Kill Devil Hills Monument area, the site of the early English colony on Roanoke Island, and most of Hatteras Island. Some of the park would be kept in a natural state for a wildlife refuge; other parts would be available for active seashore recreational pursuits. Existing villages would be excluded.

The initial steps toward this eventual goal were to get depression-era federal work programs, specifically the Civilian Conservation Corps (CCC) and the Works Progress Administration (WPA) to fund erosion control, grass planting, and dune rebuilding projects along the shore. Federal money was also sought for restoration of the "Cittie of Raleigh" and additional work at the Wright Memorial. The benefits would be two-fold: jobs for North Carolinians and conservation of Outer Banks' resources.

Many civic leaders, including state and county officials, were enthusiastically behind the plan. Some residents had doubts. It took lots of public meetings, much negotiation and the determined effort of its supporters, but finally on August 17, 1937, with the strong backing of the state of North Carolina and the support of the National Park Service, the law authorizing the Cape Hatteras National Seashore was enacted.

That was only the first step. The legislation prohibited the federal government from buying land for park purposes. It had to be donated or bought with donated money. The state of North Carolina was designated to receive and hold lands and funds until there was enough to make a national park viable.

The seashore's proponents worked diligently over the next 15 years seeking donations from private individuals, foundations, and the state. They faced many obstacles, not the least of which was that for a short period during World War II, the support of many local landowners was lost when oil companies sought leases for oil exploration in the offshore waters. Eventually things fell into place, sufficient land was acquired and the seashore became a reality when it was formally established by order of the Secretary of the Interior on January 12, 1953.

Cape Hatteras National Seashore Today

Seventy-five miles of beach facing the Atlantic Ocean await the beach walker, sunbather, swimmer, shell collector, surfer, and fisherman at Cape Hatteras National Seashore. Even on holiday weekends, there is room for everyone.

The scenery is magnificent. Waves generated hundreds of miles at sea strike the beach gently, vigorously, or furiously, depending on the weather and time of year. Seagulls—laughing, ring-billed, and great black-backs, swoop and shriek overhead. Shore-birds—willets, piping plovers, black skimmers, sanderlings—search for food on the beach or at the water's edge. Crabs and clams burrow in the sand. Beach grasses wave in the dunes.

This is a land of constant change. One day, blowing sands expose artifacts, parts of ships or cargo, long buried. Another day they are covered up again. The remains of the schooner, *Laura A. Barnes,* wrecked on Bodie Island in 1921, can be seen at Coquina Beach.

Year-round, there is teeming birdlife. Over 265 species of birds, some on the endangered species list, are regular visitors to the beaches and marshes of the seashore.

The ocean waters draw avid fishermen in spring and fall.

Historical events of the Outer Banks are commemorated at various installations, both at the seashore and in adjacent communities.

To take full advantage of all that awaits at Cape Hatteras the visitor needs several days.

How To Get There

There are two ways to get to the seashore—across bridges at the north end or by car ferries at the southern end. Coming from Norfolk, Virginia, on U.S. Route 17, take U.S. 158 from Elizabeth City, North Carolina, which crosses Currituck Sound to Kitty Hawk, 15 miles north of the entrance to the seashore. U.S. Route 64 from U.S. I-95 will take you across Croatan Sound, Roanoke Island and Roanoke Sound to the seashore's Whalebone Junction Information Center, four miles south of Nags Head.

Ferries from Cedar Island, N.C. and Swanquarter, N.C. take you to Ocracoke, a small village that retains the charm of a fishing village of years gone by. Reservations are necessary. Allow at least 2½ hours for the ferry trip. State Route 12 runs the entire length of the seashore. A bridge crosses Oregon Inlet and a free 40 minute ferry ride takes the visitor from Hatteras Island to Ocracoke Island.

Where To Stay

Private Accommodations Accommodations of all sorts are available. Hotels, motels, rental cottages and apartments, tourist homes, and campgrounds abound in the communities north of the seashore: Nags Head, Kill Devil Hills, Kitty Hawk, Duck, and Roanoke Island. The eight villages within the seashore, Rodanthe, Waves, Salvo, Avon, Buxton, Frisco, and Hatteras on Hatteras Island, and Ocracoke on Ocracoke Island have facilities of a more modest nature. Terms of seashore legislation limit village boundaries so they have not expanded to match their neighbors to the north.

Seashore Camping The seashore maintains four campgrounds on the ocean side: Oregon Inlet, Cape Point,

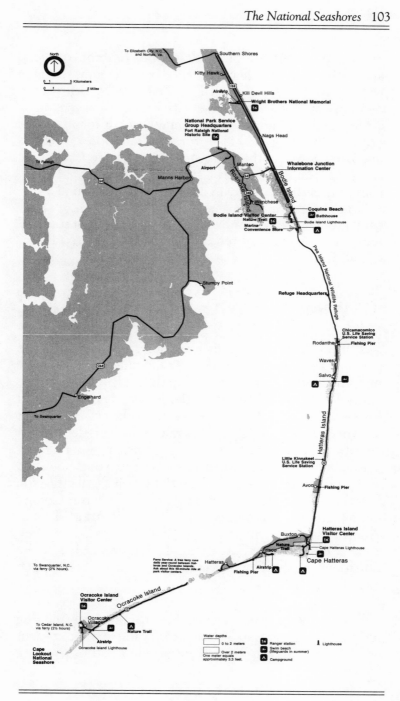

North

0 1   5 Kilometers
0   5 Miles

To Elizabeth City, N.C.
and Norfolk, Va.

Southern Shores

Kitty Hawk

Airstrip   Kill Devil Hills
158   Wright Brothers National Memorial

National Park Service
Group Headquarters
Fort Raleigh National
Historic Site
                    Nags Head

To Raleigh

Airport   Manteo
                      Whalebone Junction
                      Information Center

Manns Harbor

Roanoke Island

Wanchese
                      Coquina Beach
Bodie Island Visitor Center   Bathhouse
Nature Trail   Bodie Island Lighthouse
Marina
Convenience Store

Bodie Island

Stumpy Point

Pea Island National Wildlife Refuge

Refuge Headquarters

Chicamacomico
U.S. Life Saving
Service Station
Rodanthe   Fishing Pier

Waves

Salvo

Engelhard

To Swanquarter

Hatteras Island

Little Kinnakeet
U.S. Life Saving
Service Station

Avon   Fishing Pier

Hatteras Island
Visitor Center
Buxton
                   Cape Hatteras Lighthouse
Frisco   Nature
         Trail
Hatteras   Cape Hatteras
         Airstrip
Fishing Pier

To Swanquarter, N.C.,
via ferry (2½ hours).

Ferry Service: A free ferry runs
daily year-round between Hatteras and Ocracoke Islands.
Ask about this 40-minute ride at
park visitor centers.

Ocracoke Island

Ocracoke Island
Visitor Center

Ocracoke
Village
To Cedar Island, N.C.
via ferry (2½ hours)   Nature Trail

Airstrip
Ocracoke Island Lighthouse

Cape
Lookout
National
Seashore

Water depths
0 to 2 meters   Ranger station   Lighthouse
Over 2 meters   Swim beach
One meter equals   (lifeguards in summer)
approximately 3.3 feet.   Campground

Frisco, and Ocracoke. All are equipped for tents, trailers, and motor homes. They have modern restrooms, potable water, unheated showers, grills, and tables. No utility connections are available. Reservations for camping space during the busy summer months may be made for all except Frisco by writing to Ticketron, at Ticketron outlets in major cities and, in the summer, at the seashore. Campsites are available at Frisco on a first-come, first-served basis. Camping is allowed only in designated campgrounds.

For current information about camping sites, campground opening and closing dates, length of stay and fees, write the Superintendent of the Cape Hatteras National Seashore.

What To Do At Cape Hatteras

If you have not already sent for information from the national seashore, stop at the Whalebone Junction Information Center at the north end of the park or at one of the seashore visitor centers at Bodie Island, Hatteras Island (Buxton) or Ocracoke. At each of these places, rangers will answer questions and give you a map and a newsletter with current information about places to go and summer ranger-conducted programs. They can also tell you about the Wright Brothers National Memorial at Kill Devil Hills, the Fort Raleigh National Historic Site, the Lost Colony drama, and the Elizabethan Gardens on Roanoke Island. Another source of information is the Aycock Brown Welcome Center located on Route 158 as you arrive at the north end of the Outer Banks. Visitor centers are open daily from 9 a.m. to 5 p.m.

The Beaches The beaches are constantly moving naturally. It is estimated they are eroding at a rate of four to seven feet a year. To prevent acceleration of this rate through destruction of sand-holding grasses, use only designated access paths, boardwalks, and parking areas. Because of strong currents and shifting underwater sands, the seashore recommends swimming only where lifeguards are on duty. During the summer season, they are at Coquina Beach, Cape Point near Cape Hatteras lighthouse, and at Ocracoke near the Ocracoke airport.

Fishing And Hunting There is excellent fishing at Cape Hatteras—in the surf at beaches and inlets, from fishing piers, in freshwater ponds, from boats in inlets, the sound, and offshore. No license is required for saltwater fishing.

Sea mullet (whiting), sea trout, king and Spanish mackerel, striped bass, channel bass, bluefish, ocean perch, flounder, and tarpon, among others, can be caught depending on the season. Fishing piers are at Rodanthe, Avon, and Frisco. Public ramps for boat launching are available at a marina at Oregon Inlet and private ramps can be found in Ocracoke Village.

Charter boats run out of marinas at Oregon Inlet, Hatteras Village, and Ocracoke Village. Supplies are available in village stores and at piers. Detailed information can be obtained from seashore headquarters.

Duck hunting is permitted in the fall in accordance with the regulations of the state of North Carolina. Check with park headquarters on specific hunt regulations in the national seashore.

The Pea Island Wildlife Refuge One of the objectives of the promoters of a national seashore at the Outer Banks was to save a portion of the banks as a natural preserve, a place where birds and animals are welcomed. Work toward this goal started very early when Pea Island National Wildlife Refuge was established in 1938 within the seashore's designated boundaries. The refuge, which gets its name from the dune peas that grow in the dunes, begins at Oregon Inlet and extends south for 12 miles. Originally created to provide a winter haven for greater snow geese and other migratory waterfowl, it now provides a nesting place and feeding grounds for songbirds, shorebirds, herons, pelicans, osprey, peregrine falcons, barn owls, snow geese, and other birds, reptiles, and aquatic mammals.

Strict regulations apply to visitor activities in the area but there are observation platforms, self-guiding nature trails, and blinds permitting photographers to get close to their subjects. Walks and educational programs are led by refuge staff. For a calendar of wildlife events at Pea Island Wildlife Refuge, write the Refuge Manager.

Nature Trails Walking on trails along ponds and through woodlands are pursuits to be enjoyed at the seashore any time of the year. A trip to Bodie Island Visitor Center can include a short walk around a pond where nature strikes its own balance. Trail markers describe the life around you.

The widest part of the seashore is on Hatteras Island between Cape Point and Buxton. About halfway between on slightly elevated ground is a true maritime forest. Protected by its distance from the ocean's salt spray, pines, live oak, and hollies form a canopy cooling a .75 mile trail. Shade-tolerant shrubs, dogwoods, sweet bay, and red bay meet the eye. Interpretive trail markers explain the how and why of what you are seeing. After the open beach, the Buxton woods offers a surprising, contrasting experience.

Just beyond the entrance to the Ocracoke Campground lies Hammock Hills Nature Trail, a path through forest, salt marsh, and sand dunes.

If you are driving to Ocracoke from the north, you may want to stop at an observation platform seven miles from Ocracoke village for a look at the ponies of the Outer Banks. Once allowed to roam freely on the banks, the ponies are now confined to a penned area where their welfare is carefully monitored by seashore staff.

Oversand Vehicles (ORVs) Oversand vehicles that have a current state registration and are driven by licensed drivers may be driven on both ocean and sound beaches. Only designated ramps may be used to reach the beach. At certain times of the year, such as bird nesting and turtle nesting seasons, ORVs are prohibited in posted areas. ORVs are prohibited at all times on Pea Island Wildlife Refuge beaches. For details of rules that apply to driving on the beach, send to the seashore for a copy of *Off-Road Driving, Guide to Cape Hatteras National Seashore*.

Pets Pets must be on a leash no longer than six feet. They are prohibited on designated swimming beaches and in public eating places and food stores in the villages.

Historic/Cultural Resources Despite the loss of many historic places and artifacts to the moving sands, there remain twenty-six structures within the seashore that are now on or have been nominated to the National Register of Historic Places. They include lighthouses, keeper's quarters, life-saving stations, and the original Hatteras Weather Bureau Station.

The seashore is constantly engaged in preserving exterior features while renovating the interiors for adaptive use—such as visitor centers. The Chicamacomico Life-Saving Station may be visited at certain times in the summer. Displays depict the life of the surfmen and the boat used in the famous World War II rescue of the men of the British ship *Mirlo* is on the site.

Whenever funds become available, probably through donations, the Little Kinnakeet Life-Saving Station, located in a remote area more typical of actual life-saving station environments in the late 1800s, will be renovated and opened to the public.

Cape Hatteras—What Of The Future?

Cape Hatteras has been a bellwether for national seashores. The first to be established, the seashore has served as proving grounds for efforts to bend nature's will to fit man's desires. Year after year the federal government engaged in a major campaign to counteract the natural onslaughts of the sea on a developed coastal area. In time, the enormous costs and the futility of such efforts had to be acknowledged. The seashore is no longer trying to stabilize the shoreline.

Today, for different reasons, many people have a stake in the seashore: beach-loving vacationers, persons who make their homes and livelihoods there, the scientific community studying and learning about seashore ecology, and environmental activists seeking to preserve the islands' native resources. At times their interests conflict and hard decisions have to be made. Even then winners and losers alike agree that saving the natural, historic treasure that is Cape Hatteras National Seashore should be a high national priority.

For More Information, Contact:

Superintendent
Cape Hatteras National Seashore
Route 1, Box 675
Manteo, NC 27954
Phone: 919/473–2111

Manager
Pea Island National Wildlife Refuge
c/o Alligator River National Wildlife Refuge
P.O. Box 1969
Manteo, NC 27954
Phone 919/473-1131

Director, Ferry Division
NC Department of Transportation
Room 120, Maritime Building
113 Arendell St.
Morehead City, NC 28557
Ferries to Ocracoke from Cedar Island
and Swanquarter, NC
Ocracoke: 919/928-3841
Cedar Island: 919/225-3551
Swanquarter: 919/926-1111

Dare County Tourist Bureau
P.O. Box 399
Manteo, NC 27954
Phone: 919/473-2138

Ticketron, Dept. R
401 Hackensack Ave.
Hackensack, NJ 07601

Cape Lookout National Seashore

"The sea produced these islands, and the plants and animals that live here have adjusted themselves to the harsh environment. The islands and the life thereon will maintain themselves best if man interferes least. For the most part, man is a visitor who does not remain."

Management philosophy of
Cape Lookout National Seashore

The low, narrow ribbons of sand, sparsely vegetated, that make up the islands of Cape Lookout National Seashore—Portsmouth Island, Core Banks, and Shackleford Banks—have indeed had their visitors. Some, not many, stayed for a few generations, eking out a living from the sea. They were a hardy lot, these "Bankers." They lived on islands that, except for a few high sand dunes, are all within the 100 year flood-plain. They prospered when the sea was beneficent, and, for a time, they fought back when it wasn't. But in the end, the sea prevailed and the people left.

Family cemeteries remain. A light to warn seafarers of the shoals off Lookout Point still beams from an unmanned lighthouse. A hundred wild horses run free on Shackleford Banks. A few village structures—homes, the post office, the schoolhouse, the church—still stand, well preserved, in the little village of Portsmouth at the northern tip of the seashore—across Ocracoke Inlet from the village of Ocracoke.

Strolling on a quiet path through Portsmouth village, past the old life-saving station, across the tidal flats to the beach, you can sense the essence of island living. And wonder about the independent, proud spirit of those who dared to live there.

The islands are links in a chain of islands off the North Carolina coast called "Outer Banks."[1] The islands of Cape Lookout, however, are as different from most of the rest as day from night. There are no bridges to them, no paved roads, no motels, condominiums, restaurants, or fast-food places, and no year-round human inhabitants. Only shorebirds, a few animals, and various forms of sea life inhabit the beaches, dunes, salt marshes, flat grasslands, and the few hammocks of dense vegetation.

Except for Portsmouth Village, most of the physical evidence of former residents is gone. Some of it—abandoned cars and trucks, and shanties used by fishermen and hunters—has been removed by the seashore administration. A few structures are in occasional use under special agreements. The rest has been destroyed by fire or succumbed to wind and wave action as the sea once again staked its claim.

---

[1] The term "Outer Banks," refers to the chain of North Carolina barrier islands extending southward from the Virginia border to Shackleford Banks.

Cape Lookout National Seashore is next to the smallest of all seashores in total acreage—28,400 acres. The islands vary in width from 600 feet to 1.75 miles. They are one of the few places where you can view sand dunes never disturbed by man. Winds come from the northeast in autumn and winter, the southwest at other times, constantly reshaping the land. The islands are migrating toward the mainland as the shores erode on the ocean side an average of 1.5 feet a year.

Cape Lookout National Seashore has the smallest staff of all the seashores, the smallest budget and not many visitors—about 100,000 a year. To get there, you have to plan. You need to check out the ferry schedules, bring your own food and water, and prepare for weather changes. But for those who find pleasure in taking a solitary walk on a remote beach, primitive camping, ocean fishing, waterfowl hunting, or touching base with a vignette of maritime history, this seashore is a prize.

The Islands Before The National Seashore

Coree Indians once inhabited Shackleford Banks and Lookout Point, but most of what is known about life on the islands of Cape Lookout National Seashore starts with the eighteenth century. While the Outer Banks islands paralleling the North Carolina coast served as protective barriers from the onslaughts of the sea, they and the shallow inlets through them were an obstacle to ships transporting commercial products to and from the mainland.

In 1753 the legislature authorized the establishment of the town of Portsmouth on the southern border of Ocracoke Inlet to help solve this problem. Here, it was planned, the cargo of heavily-laden ships could be unloaded and stored in warehouses, then transported to the growing cities along the coast in lighter, shallow draft boats. (The term "lightering" is used to describe this procedure.) The larger ships, unburdened of much of their cargo, could then proceed through the inlet. Early on, private interests built warehouses on nearby Shell Castle Island (made up entirely of oyster shells) which became the prime storage area.

For nearly 100 years, the pilots and other residents of Portsmouth derived their livelihood from the work involved in this operation or the support of those who were. The town also was the site of a marine hospital and, for a brief period, a small fort.

During the Civil War, most residents fled Portsmouth and Confederate and Union troops each spent time there. After the war, some residents came back but the fickleness of the sea, upon which the town's prosperity was dependent, settled its fate. A better inlet had broken through at Hatteras Inlet during a mid-century storm. Major commercial shipping no longer passed through Ocracoke Inlet and the economic well-being of Portsmouth came to an end.

To the south, in and along the Core Banks, Lookout Point, Lookout Bight, and Shackleford Banks, maritime-related activity was of a different sort.

Nature did not provide the early island settlers with soil for a bountiful harvest of land crops, but she was generous when it came to food from the sea. Early colonists engaged in "the taking of whales." At first their methods were primitive. A 1709 account relates: "Whales are very numerous on the coast of North Carolina . . . where these Whales come ashore, none being struck or killed with a Harpoon in the Place, as they are to the Northward . . . ; all those Fish being found dead on the Shoar, most common-ly by those that inhabit the banks and sea-side where they dwell . . ."

New England whalers frequented the waters of North Carolina. Some of them decided to settle down in the area. Soon the local fishermen, at first perhaps guided by the ex-perienced New Englanders, were taking to their boats and hunting for their prey. After a whale was killed, it was towed to the beach where try-pots were set up for boiling the blubber as the whale was cut up.

The whalers liked to name the whales. One was called "Mayflower" because it was caught on May 4. Another was called "Haint Bin Named Yet."

The town of Diamond City on the east end of Shack-leford Banks for a time thrived as the center of North Carolina whaling. Eventually the waters along the coast were whaled out and by 1900, battered both by the loss of a productive livelihood and a severe hurricane, everyone had gone. Some took their houses with them to Harker's Is-land, Beaufort, Morehead City, and Salter Path.

Cape Lookout Bight is a natural fish trap and around the turn of the century mullet fishing was an active com-mercial enterprise. From June until late fall, crews of mul-let fishermen set up their operations on the Outer Banks, fanning out with their nets to catch the fish on both the sound and ocean sides as they migrated northward. Commercial fishing is still important to the economy of coastal North Carolina.

Early seafarers sailing along the North Carolina coast both feared and appreciated the configuration of Cape Lookout. On the one hand, dangerous shoals extended out from the cape about 10 miles. Low lying land and frequent fog hampered visibility, adding to the hazardous conditions. "Promontorium tremendum," horrible headland, was what Cape Lookout was termed by a late sixteenth century map maker.

But if a vessel safely traversed the perilous waters and made it around the sandy point that curved to the west, forming Lookout Bight, a safe harbor awaited. This spot became a favored rendezvous site for fighting ships from pirates and Spanish privateers to British warships in the American Revolution and the War of 1812. Union ships planning blockades of southern ports during the Civil War and Europe-bound convoys of World Wars I and II also rendezvoused there.

Responding at last to the long-known hazards of the shoals off Cape Lookout, Congress authorized the building of a lighthouse. It was completed in 1812. It was not the most effective lighthouse on the Atlantic coast and there were many complaints about its poor visibility and lighting system. By 1859, a new tower had been built and a "state-of-the-art" Fresnel lens installed. In 1873 a distinctive black and white diagonal checker[2] design was painted on the tower, serving as a useful day marker, which it does to this day. In 1950, the lighthouse, by then under the jurisdiction of the U.S. Coast Guard, was automated.

For those whose ships did not find safe passage, there was one last hope. As on other key barrier islands, courageous men, members of the U.S. Life-Saving Service, frequently risked their lives in daring rescue efforts. For about fifty years, starting in the late 1800s, they braved the

[2] Often called "diamond."

perils of the sea and, from three life-saving stations—at Portsmouth, at Cape Lookout, and about halfway between on Core Banks—they rowed their surfboats through stormy seas to save the crews of foundering ships.

Core Banks may have been sparsely populated in the early decades of the twentieth century, but it was not forgotten. Because of its particular location along the Atlantic coast and the excellent harbor at Lookout Bight, at different times the island was of special significance to shipping interests, the military, and fishermen.

After many years of study to determine the best location for a "Harbor Of Refuge" for large vessels facing severe weather along the Carolina coast, in 1914 work began on the construction of an extensive stone breakwater further enclosing Lookout Bight. The prospect of turning Cape Lookout into a major seaport brightened with the news that the Norfolk and Southern Railway Company planned to extend the rail line from Beaufort to Shackleford Banks and over to Cape Lookout if the federal government built the breakwater.

Work stopped on the project before it was completed, however, when World War I erupted. It was never finished and plans to extend the railroad to the banks were dropped.

World War II was a very real and present danger to people living on the banks. The sights and sounds of warfare on the seas were with them constantly in the early months of the war when German U-Boats prowled the coastal waters, sometimes scoring direct hits on American merchant ships.

The Army placed guns at strategic points to protect the entrance to the harbor at Cape Lookout; Coast Guard cutters patrolled the ocean; and volunteers backed them up. Some flew Civil Air Patrol planes and some, members of the Home Guard, used their own boats to patrol the coastal waters and perform whatever tasks the Navy asked of them.

Those were the bad times; but between wars, there were lots of good times. It was a favored spot for many North Carolina mainlanders to vacation. The fishing was great at the point, near the abandoned breakwater, and further north at Drum Inlet. Private and "party" boats congregated, especially on weekends. After the fishing, there was square dancing and listening to songs sung by favorite balladeers.

Recreational fishermen and hunters came in increasing numbers to the shores of Core and Shackleford Banks after World War II. The regulars built overnight shanties, some on land they did not own. They ferried cars, trucks, and oversand vehicles to the islands so they could follow their prey. When the cars broke down, they were abandoned and parts of the islands looked like junkyards.

The Making Of The Cape Lookout National Seashore

In the sixties, officials of the state of North Carolina looked into the feasibility of creating a state park on Cape Lookout. They concluded it would be too expensive. Yet the islands offered a rare opportunity to establish a public recreational site in a remote, predominantly natural maritime environment. The National Park Service was approached, North Carolina's Congressmen introduced the legislation and in May 1966, Cape Lookout National Seashore was authorized.

In the twenty years that followed, the seashore took on two major tasks. First, a clean-up operation. Twenty-five hundred abandoned vehicles and over 300 "squatter" dwellings had to be removed from the sands and grasslands. Marine helicopters were called in to airlift rusted cars and trucks to acceptable disposal sites. Deteriorating structures were torn down and burned. By the beginning of 1986, the job was done and most of the land reverted to its natural, sea-buffeted state.

Equally important was the second project—acting quickly to acquire and preserve the remaining structures of the village of Portsmouth so that the village could be restored and serve as an authentic, living demonstration of the daily life of the Bankers in the early days of the twentieth century. This task, well under way, is ongoing.

Cape Lookout National Seashore Today

The last three permanent residents left in 1971, but a few of the former residents retain the right to use their houses during their lifetimes. They often return to the village for short stays in good weather. Some serve as volunteer National Park Service guides. They welcome your questions about life on a remote island with no telephone or electricity but plenty of seafood and self-created entertainment. When you go there, if you see a gentle, smiling lady sitting on her front porch, enjoying the cool sea breezes, stop by and visit. She'll tell you the returnees agree that "Being here is like going to heaven without dying."

How To Get There

Access to all parts of Cape Lookout National Seashore is by ferry or private boat only. Up-to-date, detailed information about island conditions can be obtained from seashore rangers at three places—the temporary Cape Lookout National Seashore Headquarters at Beaufort, North Carolina, the temporary visitor center on Harker's Island, or at the visitor center at Ocracoke, a unit of the Cape Hatteras National Seashore.

Beaufort is on U.S. Route 70, 100 miles east of U.S. I-95. If traveling by boat, use the Intracoastal Waterway which passes near Beaufort. To get to the Harker's Island Visitor Center, leave route 70 about halfway between Otway and Smyrna and take SR 1332 and SR 1335 south for eight miles. Ocracoke is at the southern tip of Cape Hatteras National Seashore, on State Route 12.

If your destination is Portsmouth, take a boat from Ocracoke. Reservations are necessary. Information about

schedules and fees can be obtained from seashore headquarters or at the Cape Hatteras Visitor Center at Ocracoke. When you return to Ocracoke, if you want to visit other parts of Cape Lookout, take the car ferry to Cedar Island. Reservations are necessary. The ferry lands at SR 12 which leads to U.S. Route 70.

Ferries to the lighthouse, the Lookout Bight area, and Shackleford Banks run from Harker's Island. Ferries equipped to transport four-wheel drive vehicles run from Davis to near Great Island, Core Banks, and from Atlantic to an area north of Drum Inlet. From Drum Inlet, it is possible to drive in a four-wheel drive vehicle to Portsmouth. Davis and Atlantic are on Route 70.

Ferries operate from spring until fall at specified times. Round trip prices range from $10.00 per person to $40.00 for one to three persons in a group; vehicles, $50.00. Permits are required to take a vehicle to Core Banks. They are free and may be obtained from seashore headquarters or the ferry operators. No motorized vehicles are allowed on Shackleford Banks. All ferries are operated by seashore concessioners. For ferry schedules, rates, and regulations applying to car transport, write to the Superintendent, Cape Lookout National Seashore.

Where To Stay

You have a choice. For a primitive overnight stay, you can bring all your supplies, including water, and pitch a tent on the islands or you can stay in one of the few simple structures available for rent by concessioners. For information and advice about overnighting on the islands, contact seashore headquarters.

Private Accommodations There are several motels in Beaufort, a lovely, old coastal town where the seashore's administrative headquarters is located. Harker's Island and Ocracoke also have accommodations. For information, write to the Carteret County Chamber of Commerce. The North Carolina Travel and Tourism Division, Department of Commerce also publishes an *Accommodations Directory.* The directory lists many hostelries that are locally-owned. For information about motels operated by major chains, check their directories, available on request.

Camping The Carteret County Chamber of Commerce provides information about drive-in campgrounds in the vicinity of the seashore and the North Carolina Travel and Tourism Division will send you a copy of its *Camping and Outdoors Directory* on request.

What To Do At Cape Lookout

Go prepared. There is little shade or shelter on the islands. The only comfort station is near the lighthouse and there are three shade shelters at various points on Core Banks. Take a shirt and hat and an effective sunscreen lotion to protect you from the sun, and insect repellent to ward off biting insects. Bring food and drink. There is no reliable source of palatable water.

Take a container for the great variety of seashells you will find and binoculars for a better view of wildlife. Remember the hour the ferry leaves for the return trip. When you leave, do your part to keep Cape Lookout an unspoiled seashore and take your trash with you.

Once you are there, you are pretty much on your own. If you go to Portsmouth, take a brochure from a box near the boat landing. It will serve as your guide on a walk through the village. Beyond the former U.S. Life-Saving Station at the edge of town, a sign will point to a path for a mile-long walk over the tidal flats to the pristine beach.

Here you can sunbathe, swim, surf, picnic, fish, gather treasures from the sea, or fantasize about life on a deserted island.

If you are a bird watcher, in spring and fall look for migrating birds; in summer, terns, black skimmers, plovers, egrets, and heron nest at the seashore. At times, you can see the eastern brown pelican and the peregrine falcon, both on the endangered species list. Atlantic loggerhead turtles, on the list of threatened species, come up on the beaches at nesting time. Visitors will be warned to stay away from these areas when this occurs.

Do not pick sea oats. The spreading roots of these golden tasseled grasses hold the sand and are one of the few natural stabilizing forces. They are protected by law.

The ferry from Harker's Island lands a short distance from the dramatic diamond-patterned Cape Lookout Lighthouse. During the summer, a ranger will be on the island and will gladly tell you about the geology of the island and its natural and social history. Feel free to ask questions. As yet, no special facilities exist for access to the islands by the handicapped.

Programs about the natural and cultural history of the seashore are offered twice daily in the vicinity of the lighthouse complex in summer. The lighthouse is still an active aid to navigation and is not open to the public.

Walk on both the sound and ocean sides of the island and observe the difference in sand and sea life on the shores. If you want to go out to Lookout Point where shell-collecting is particularly appealing, you can take the three mile walk along the beach or ride the motorized jitney the concessioner operates. The cost is $2.50 per person each way.

For variation in scenery, you may choose to visit Shackleford Banks which is an eight mile island running east to west. Facing the prevailing winds, the blowing sand builds the dunes as high as 35 feet. Behind them, near the western end of the island, is a maritime forest.

The designation of Shackleford Banks as an official wilderness area is under consideration. Until such action is taken, the island is being managed as a natural zone. There are no facilities and no motorized vehicles are allowed. Wild horses run free.

Hunting And Fishing You may want to fish or hunt migrating waterfowl. Among the fish most sought are drum, speckled trout, flounder, bluefish, Spanish mackerel, and pompano. No license is required for salt water fishing. Hunting and fishing regulations of the state of North Carolina apply. For details contact North Carolina's Department of Natural Resources and Community Development, Wildlife Resources Commission.

Oversand Vehicles (ORVs) All vehicles on Core Banks, including oversand vehicles, must be driven only on designated paths so that the least harm will be done to the environment.

Pets Pets are prohibited on the ferry boats. They may be taken to the island in private boats so long as they are on a leash when other visitors are near.

Cape Lookout—An Undiscovered Delight

Residents of the state of North Carolina have been coming to Cape Lookout for many years in their own boats to fish, hunt, or just to "get away from it all." Unlike most national seashores, this one is yet to be discovered by beach lovers from the rest of the nation. A mild, sunny climate makes the seashore enjoyable from spring to late fall. Travelers driving the north-south corridor of the East coast will find it worthwhile to detour to Cape Lookout for a day and step back in time to a period when man generally accepted nature as he found it.

For More Information, Contact:

Superintendent
Cape Lookout National Seashore
P.O. Box 690
Beaufort, NC 28516
Phone: 919/728–2121

NC Travel and Tourism Division
430 N. Salisbury St.
Raleigh, NC 27603
Phone: 1/800/VISITNC

Carteret County Chamber of Commerce
P.O. Box 1198
Morehead City, N.C. 28557
Phone: 919/726–6831
1/800/NC-COAST

Ferries between Cedar Island and Ocracoke:
Ocracoke: phone 919/928–3841
Cedar Island: phone 919/225–3551

North Carolina Dept. of Natural Resources
and Community Development
Wildlife Resources Commission
512 N. Salisbury St.
Raleigh, N.C. 27611–7687
Phone: 919/733–7191

Cumberland Island National Seashore

"Cumberland Island is a place that nourishes the spirit, rejuvenates energies, and may lead to the rediscovery of one's soul."

— Stephen R. Swinburne,

Guide to Cumberland Island National Seashore

Tacatacoru—Missoe—San Pedro—Cumberland—Dungeness. These island names reflect the cultural heritage of the people who, in their own time, drew on Cumberland Island's rich land and maritime resources to fill their special needs.

Prehistoric Indians subsisted on the bounty of the hunt: deer, bear, and wildfowl, and great varieties of fish, especially shellfish. The Spanish built a fort to protect their colonizing efforts and sent missionaries to convert the Indians. The British reached out from their Georgia mainland bases to challenge the Spanish for possession of the coastal islands. The Americans lumbered and worked plantations and when these ventures were no longer profitable, wealthy businessmen took over and used the island as a private retreat for their own recreational pursuits.

Now Cumberland Island is a national seashore. Some residences and lands are still in private ownership. One spacious island home is currently operated as an inn by its octogenarian owner whose family has been on the island for over a century. But most of this enchanting isle is there for all beach lovers, campers, and hikers to enjoy, in limited numbers, year-round.

Cumberland Island is the largest and southernmost of the Sea Islands off the coast of Georgia. It is broader, more stable, and more lush in vegetation than the Outer Banks Islands of North Carolina. The area known as Big Cumberland Island, the site of the seashore, is approximately 16 miles long and varies in width from .5 miles near the southern tip to 3 miles.

The Cumberland River and Cumberland Sound, part of the Intracoastal Waterway, separate the island from the mainland. On the south, the entrance to St. Marys River divides it from Amelia Island in Florida. To the north lies Little Cumberland Island across salt marshes and Christmas Creek. Technically within the boundaries of the seashore, Little Cumberland Island is being maintained as a natural preserve by the island's private property owners under terms of an irrevocable trust. So long as the trust is not violated, the federal government will not acquire land on Little Cumberland Island. To the east is the Atlantic Ocean.

Wide, sweeping beaches gradually slope into the ocean on the east side of the island. One prominent dune ridge, up to 40 feet in some places, extends north to south on most of the island. Fresh water ponds, fertile salt marshes, and cool, dense, maritime forests support a rich variety of animal, seabird, plant, and marine life.

Though the island is subject to a modest amount of erosion due to the worldwide rise in sea level and blowing winter winds, it rarely is subjected to the devastating effects of violent maritime storms. The mild temperatures characteristic of southern coastal islands attract visitors in all seasons.

Cumberland Island Before The National Seashore

By the time the Spanish pushed north from their colonial bases on the Florida coast in the 1560s, Timucuan Indians had been living along the Georgia coast for three to four thousand years. They made pottery and fashioned tools and decorative ornaments from shells. They hunted and fished and traveled in canoes. Cumberland Island was a hospitable place and the Tacatacoru tribe of Timucuans settled on Missoe, an Indian name for the island.

The Spanish built a fort on the island and called it San Pedro. They were not welcomed by the Tacatacorus and the first missionaries, the Jesuits, failed in their efforts to convert the natives to Christianity. But twenty years later the Franciscans took over mission work and by the beginning of the seventeenth century, the Indians were loyal, converted friends.

The English came to Cumberland Island as a consequence of their several decades of conflict with the Spanish to determine which nation would control the colonizing of the Georgia-Florida coast. When the English staked their claim, they called the island Cumberland, a name suggested by an Indian who had been cordially treated by the Duke of Cumberland when his English friend, Colonel James Oglethorpe, took him to London.

Forts were built on the north and south ends of the island and by 1763 the English had clearly won out.

The first "Dungeness" was built during this period. Named for a royal estate on the Cape of Dungeness in Kent, the structure is believed to have been used in connection with the hunt for food for troops at Fort Prince William at South Point. Later islanders referred to the building as Oglethorpe's "hunting lodge."

Life was quiet on the island until General Nathanael Greene, outstanding American military leader in the

Revolutionary War, bought a sizeable piece of land on the south end. It is believed he intended to harvest live oak timber for shipbuilding and build a family home there. He died before the home was built but his widow, Catherine, had a four story mansion constructed of tabby, a mixture of shells, lime, sand, and water. Twelve acres of flower gardens and tropical plants including dates, guavas, olives, and oranges surrounded the house. Under the supervision of Phineas Miller, Catherine Greene's second husband, the estate, called Dungeness, became one of the island's first major plantations, growing cotton and sugar cane.

The nineteenth century saw great changes on Cumberland Island. Until the outbreak of the Civil War, the island thrived primarily on lumbering and farming. Live oak timber was considered a prime material for shipbuilding. Plantations supplied high-grade long staple cotton. Hogs, cattle, and horses were kept and food was grown for island inhabitants, including the numerous slaves essential to the plantation economy. Shell middens were tapped to build a base for a road running the length of the island and to form an essential ingredient of tabby.

Prosperity ended with the Civil War and the loss of slave labor. Many plantations deteriorated, including Dungeness. Property began to change hands, the purchasers being people of means seeking private recreational retreats. Most well-known among the new landowners was Thomas M. Carnegie of the wealthy steel-producing family who came to the island in 1881. He built a grand and glorious new Dungeness on the former Nathanael Greene property. He and his wife, Lucy Coleman Carnegie, enjoyed life on the island so much they expanded their holdings until they owned 90 percent of the island.

Over the years the Carnegies built a nine-hole golf course, a guest home with swimming pool, island homes for their children, and roads to remote areas. They also farmed vegetables and kept hogs, cattle, and horses.

Lucy Carnegie outlived her husband by many years. Before she died in 1916, she set up a trust to maintain her Cumberland Island property as an entity for the use of all her children until the last one died.

The Making Of The Cumberland Island National Seashore

With the family's matriarch no longer on the scene, it became increasingly difficult to manage the Cumberland Island holdings. The various Carnegie heirs had different ideas. As early as the 1950s, one heir began to search for a way to save the island in its natural state for future generations to enjoy. Others sought ways to derive income from the property. Another went to court to prevent the Carnegie trust from leasing land for the mining of several kinds of ore known to be in the sands of the sea islands.

When the "last surviving child" of Lucy Carnegie died in 1962, the land was divided among the heirs. Each heir was free to make an individual decision about the future of his or her property.

Land developers began to cast their eyes on Cumberland Island. One succeeded in acquiring a small parcel and laid plans for the development of a high class resort. But more land was needed. He began to woo other property owners.

A 1956 National Park Service report had cited Cumberland Island as "one of the two most outstanding undeveloped seashore areas remaining along the Atlantic and Gulf coasts." The special attributes of Cumberland Island were also recognized by persons associated with conservation minded organizations and foundations.

The heirs who wanted to preserve Cumberland Island in a natural state entered into negotiations to transfer their property to the National Park Foundation, a private nonprofit association. The Andrew Mellon Foundation provided the funds to acquire the land and hold it for eventual donation to the federal government.

Soon after the establishment of the Cumberland Island National Seashore was authorized in 1972, about 13,000 acres of former Carnegie land was donated to the seashore by the National Park Foundation, forming the bulk of the area now owned by the seashore.

A few island tracts remain in private ownership. So long as these lands are managed in accordance with the preservation ethic of Cumberland Islanders of the past there will be no need for the federal government to acquire additional acreage.

Cumberland Island National Seashore Today

Cumberland Island is one of the National Park Systems's unexpected treasures. The same sights and sounds that drew vacationers a century ago remain for the enjoyment of seashore visitors today.

A visit to the island is an experience long remembered and one shared by only a few fortunate travelers. For in order to keep as much of the island as possible in a natural state, no more than about 300 persons are permitted to visit the national seashore at any given time. And those visitors can only get there by Park Service ferry or private boat.

Cumberland Island has special appeal for beach lovers who seek a quiet, awe-inspiring encounter with nature.

There is great beauty. A sea of tall, spindly, green to gold cordgrass borders the entire sound side, and here and there a snowy egret, white ibis, or great blue heron may be seen wading in the mud.

Centuries old live oak trees form a dark, cool sunshade over spongy brown trails traversed by hiker, white-tailed deer, nine-banded armadillo, and raccoons. Light greenish grey feathery Spanish moss drips down from massive branches to gently brush saw palmetto growing in great profusion.

Remote fresh water lakes and ponds support game fish and colorful pond lilies and attract osprey and waterfowl. In the forest, alligators, mink, and otter slip in and out of brackish sloughs (pronounced "slews").

A grand expanse of lightly colored, firmly packed sandy beach, littered with great numbers of unbroken shells, gradually slopes to meet a gentle surf.

Much of Cumberland Island remained in its primitive state when the seashore was established. In 1982 Congress designated nearly 9,000 acres in the central and northern portions as a national wilderness area. Another 11,718 acres were declared potential wilderness. These lands will become wilderness areas when all existing rights and uses incompatible with wilderness status have expired.

How To Get There

Seashore headquarters, where you board the Cumberland Queen ferry, is at St. Marys, Georgia. St. Marys is nine miles east of U.S. I-95, just north of the Florida-Georgia border.

Going to Cumberland Island National Seashore is not a quick sightseeing trip. It's an adventure that should be planned and savored. Whether going for a few hours, a full day, or several days of backpack camping, make reservations well in advance for the ferry trip and if you plan to camp, for a campsite. No food or supplies, other than water, are available on the island, so take along food, drink, sunscreen lotions, insect repellent, fishing gear, clothing for possible weather changes—whatever you may need while there.

To make reservations, both for the ferry trip and a campsite, phone the seashore reservation number 912/882-4335, between 10 a.m. and 2 p.m., Monday through Friday. At certain times the phone is extremely busy so be patient and persistent. You may also make reservations in person at seashore headquarters seven days a week.

Reservations may be made up to 11 months in advance of the dates you plan to be on the island. Be forewarned—space on the ferry fills up quickly for the period from mid-March through April and on weekends. To save time and phone call expense, write the seashore before you make reservations for information on schedules, rates, and cancellation procedure.

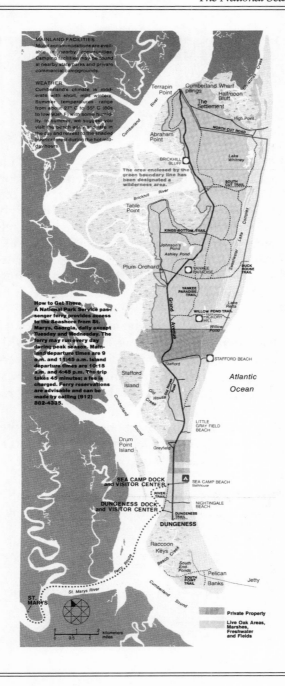

MAINLAND FACILITIES
Motel accommodations are available in nearby communities. Camping facilities may be found at nearby state parks and private commercial campgrounds.

WEATHER
Cumberland's climate is moderate with short, mild winters. Summer temperatures range from about 27° C to 35° C (60s to low 90s° F) with some humidity. In summer, we suggest you visit the beach early and hide in the day and retreat to the shaded interior forest during the hot midday hours.

The area enclosed by the green boundary line has been designated a wilderness area.

How to Get There
A National Park Service passenger ferry provides access to the Seashore from St. Marys, Georgia, daily except Tuesday and Wednesday. The ferry may run every day during peak season. Mainland departure times are 9 a.m. and 11:45 a.m. Island departure times are 10:15 a.m. and 4:45 p.m. The trip takes 45 minutes; a fee is charged. Ferry reservations are advisable and can be made by calling (912) 882-4335.

Terrapin Point

Cumberland Wharf pilings
Halfmoon Bluff
The Settlement
High Point

NORTH CUT ROAD

Abraham Point

BRICKHILL BLUFF

Lake Whitney

SOUTH CUT TRAIL

Brickhill River

Table Point

KINGS BOTTOM TRAIL

Johnson's Pond
Ashley Pond

Plum Orchard

YANKEE PARADISE

YANKEE PARADISE TRAIL

BUCK HOUSE TRAIL

WILLOW POND TRAIL

Lake Retta

HICKORY HILL

Willow Pond

Grand Avenue

STAFFORD BEACH

Atlantic Ocean

Stafford

Stafford Island

Old House Creek

Cumberland Sound

LITTLE GRAY FIELD BEACH

Drum Point Island

Greyfield

SEA CAMP DOCK and VISITOR CENTER

SEA CAMP BEACH
Bathhouse

RIVER TRAIL

NIGHTINGALE BEACH

DUNGENESS DOCK and VISITOR CENTER

DUNGENESS TRAIL

DUNGENESS

Raccoon Keys

Beach Creek

South End Pond

SOUTH POINT TRAIL

Pelican Banks

Jetty

Cumberland Sound

Ferry Route

St. Marys River

ST. MARYS

kilometers
0   0.5   1
miles

Private Property

Live Oak Areas, Marshes, Freshwater and Fields

The ferry does not run on Tuesdays and Wednesdays from Labor Day to mid-May. However, special charters may be arranged on these days for groups of 46 or more.

Where To Stay

Private Accommodations Except for camp-sites, there are no seashore facilities for overnighting on the island. The privately-owned Greyfield Inn, one of four original Carnegie homes on the island, offers the only other island accommodations. It has nine double rooms, all except one, with shared bathrooms. The rate, in the expensive range, includes three meals. For information, contact Greyfield Inn. Transportation to the inn from either Fernandina Beach or the seashore's island docks can be arranged. Advance reservations for the inn is a must.

Accommodations are available at motels along I-95. There are also facilities in the town of St. Marys, which is a picturesque, historic coastal village. The Riverview Hotel, built in an earlier era, has a number of rooms and a dining room. The Charter House Inn is of more recent vintage.

For additional information about hotels and motels in the area, write the Georgia Department of Industry and Trade, Tourist/Communications Division.

Camping A 16-site campground, allowing no more than 60 campers, is located one-half mile from Sea Camp Dock. All food and equipment must be hand-carried from the dock to the campsite. Water, cold water showers, and restrooms are available. Day use beachgoers may also use these facilities.

Maximum stay at the campsite is seven days. There is no fee. Campfires are permitted. During the summer, check posted schedules for ranger-conducted programs.

There are four primitive camping areas for backpackers. One, a 3.5 mile walk from Sea Camp, is at Stafford Beach. Three are within the National Wilderness Area at distances of 5.5, 7.4 and 10.6 miles from Sea Camp. Fires are not permitted in primitive areas. Bring a camp stove. There are no restrooms. Trash must be carried out when you leave. Twenty is the maximum number of primitive campers at any one site for a maximum of 60 at all sites.

Camping is available on the mainland at Georgia's Crooked River State Park year-round. There are spaces for motorized vehicles, pop-up campers, and tents. Water, electricity, dump stations, hot showers, grills, and picnic tables are provided. The park also has a swimming pool, a miniature golf course, and rental cabins. For information write the Superintendent, Crooked River State Park.

What To Do At Cumberland Island

Plan to arrive at seashore headquarters about one-half hour before ferry departure time so that you can get your boarding pass, watch an audio-visual presentation about the seashore, check out publications and displays, and listen to a ranger orientation talk. In warm weather, be sure to take insect repellent. "No see-ums" (very tiny, biting insects) frequent the dock area in great numbers.

After a 45 minute ride down the St. Marys River and across Cumberland Sound, you will leave the boat either at the Dungeness Dock or Sea Camp Dock. There is a visitor center at Sea Camp. It has restrooms and offers exhibits oriented to the island's natural history. A limited number of private boats may also dock for the day at Sea Camp Dock. Adjacent to the Dungeness dock there is a museum featuring the island's cultural history. The Dungeness washhouse has been renovated to provide restrooms and an interpretive center.

The Trails A few hours' visit will permit you to walk the Dungeness Trail, a loop from one dock area across the island through the forest to the beach, along the beach, and back across the island to the other dock, a distance of about 3 miles. Take along a brochure that explains the natural and man-made features along the trail. Among the sights you will see are a high dune gradually pushing across the island, sands burying palm trees in the path, and wild horses grazing in open meadows.

The last Dungeness mansion, built by the Carnegies, was destroyed by fire in 1959. Pause a while at the ruins, look at some of the estate buildings still standing, and visualize life on the island when this beautiful retreat brought joy and pleasure to a well-to-do, conservation-minded family.

If you spend the day at Cumberland, there will be time for swimming, shell collecting, picnicking, and walking on some of the many island trails, varying in length from .5 miles to 14 miles. A trail map is available at seashore head-quarters.

A word of caution. There are no lifeguards at the beach. When walking, stay on trails. Poisonous snakes, including diamondback rattlers and cottonmouth moccasins, live on the island, as do wild hogs. Over 1400 hogs have been removed by the seashore but a few still rumble through the woods and marshes.

You may be surprised to see a motorized vehicle. Seashore visitors may not take them to the island but island property holders still have the right to use their own vehicles on island roads.

A Visit To Plum Orchard Once a month—on the first Sunday of each month—the ferry makes a trip to Plum Orchard, a lovely island home built for one of Lucy Carnegie's children. The exterior of the home, which is over 85 years old, has been restored by the Park Service. Volunteers have been raising funds for interior renovation and have acquired authentic furnishings. For detailed information, write the Superintendent, Cumberland Island National Seashore.

Wildlife And Endangered Species Of high priority in the management of Cumberland Island National Seashore is the protection of native wildlife and the many endangered and threatened species that frequent the seashore. A small brochure, *Birds of Cumberland Island*, lists 277 species that have been seen on the island.

Included among the endangered or threatened species are brown pelican, Arctic peregrine falcon, American alligator, and the Loggerhead sea turtle. The seashore is engaged in a special project to observe the natural hatching process of the Loggerhead turtle. From mid-May to mid-August, female turtles emerge from the ocean and lay their eggs in nests they prepare on the beach. Visitors are asked not to disturb turtles during the nesting and incubation periods and when hatchlings emerge from the sand and make their way to the ocean. The seashore has published an interesting brochure, *Caretta Caretta Research Project*, describing details.

Hunting And Fishing As required by the seashore's enabling legislation, hunting is allowed. The seashore conducts deer hunts as part of the management of the deer population and in accordance with the hunting laws of the state of Georgia. These hunts are scheduled during certain periods in the fall and early winter. Persons permitted to take part in the hunts are determined by lottery. For detailed information, write the Superintendent,

Cumberland Island National Seashore. Only persons directly involved in the hunt are allowed in the designated areas during those times.

State laws apply to fresh water fishing. No license is needed for salt water fishing. Fish most sought by sportsmen include channel bass, flounder, speckled trout, and whiting.

Pets Pets may not be taken on ferries, so plan to leave them elsewhere when you go to Cumberland Island.

Historical/Cultural Resources A number of prehistoric and historic sites have been identified. Many specific sites have been grouped to form historic districts. Virtually all of the island's known cultural resources are on the National Register of Historic Places. They include Greyfield, Dungeness, Plum Orchard, Stafford Plantation, and High Point/Halfmoon Bluff Historic District, which includes cemeteries and a church associated with blacks who lived on the island during the plantation and turn-of-the-century periods.

Cumberland Island National Seashore—A Special Adventure

"Things just happened" is how a Carnegie descendent put it when asked how she spent her time on the island as a child. "You were always discovering something fascinating—in the sloughs,—in the woods,—on the beach." Intriguing natural events are still happening on Cumberland Island. And they are there to be "discovered" today by any visitor searching for adventure.

For More Information, Contact:

Superintendent
Cumberland Island National Seashore
P.O. Box 806
St. Marys, GA 31558
Phone: General Information 912/882–4336
Reservations 912/882–4335

Greyfield Inn
P.O. Drawer B
Fernandina Beach, FL 32034
Phone: 904/261–6408

Riverview Hotel
105 Osborne St.
St. Marys, GA 31558
Phone: 912/882–3242

St. Marys Tourism Council
P.O. Box 1291
St. Marys, GA 31558
Phone: 912/882–6200

Crooked River State Park
3092 Spur 40
St. Marys, GA 31558
Phone: 912/882–5256

Canaveral National Seashore

Wilderness and Wizardry By The Sea

M ention Cape Cod or Cape Hatteras and almost everyone visualizes vast stretches of ocean beach and cookouts on the sand. Mention Canaveral and the immediate thought is of rockets and space shuttle launches. Except for those who live in or frequently visit the central portion of eastern Florida, few people realize that Canaveral is also a national seashore that includes 24 miles of undeveloped beachfront available for year-round enjoyment by beach lovers fortunate enough to have discovered it.

Canaveral National Seashore is unique in its origin and in its relationship to other government agencies. Most of the land and waters within the seashore's boundaries are owned by the National Aeronautics and Space Administration (NASA). By special agreement, the major portion of NASA's property is managed by the Federal Fish and Wildlife Service.

There is historical reason for this juxtaposition of federal authorities, each with its own special national mission. NASA was on the scene first. In the early 1960s as its operations were expanding, NASA reached out from its restrictive Cape Canaveral base to acquire the adjacent lands on Merritt Island and built the Kennedy Space Center.

In 1963 NASA made an agreement with the Department of the Interior providing for the Department's Fish and Wildlife Service to establish and manage the Merritt Island National Wildlife Refuge on NASA land. The intent was to have the refuge serve as a buffer zone for aerospace operations at the Kennedy Space Center.

In 1975, by Congressional act, the Interior Department's National Park Service was brought into the picture. The Canaveral National Seashore was authorized primarily to provide for Park Service management of the barrier beach extending from the Kennedy Space Center north to the community of New Smyrna Beach.

Today man, nature, and high technology coexist in a fragile alliance at Canaveral National Seashore, though the law gives the space program primacy.

For the beach lover, the striking feature of the seashore is its long, thin sand barrier, the last pristine beachfront in eastern Florida, a state famous for its populous, developed beach resorts. The barrier was formed out of the sea's depths a million years ago. It consists predominantly of pure quartz sand. Though subject to littoral drifting sands and frequent overwash, the beaches are relatively stable. Beaches are fairly steep and blowing sands have built up a dune ridge to a height of about 12 feet. The marshes and lands protected by the dunes have been and continue to be reshaped by both natural and human action.

The dunes, Mosquito Lagoon, and the marshes and woodlands of Canaveral National Seashore attract a rich variety of wildlife—wading birds and marsh birds, migrating waterfowl, finfish, shellfish, reptiles, and animals.

As early as 1955 the National Park Service had its eye on this area. A survey found it to be one of sixteen prime spots along the Atlantic and Gulf coasts still available for public recreation. A subtropical climate attracted people in every season. Close proximity to major transportation networks and a variety of nearby vacation destinations added to its appeal. But in the national balance that had to be struck, NASA got there first and it wasn't until 20 years later that a choice parcel of beaches and waters of eastern Florida became part of the National Park System.

Canaveral Before The National Seashore

Though the beach was undisturbed when the federal government took over, evidence exists of previous users of Canaveral's land and waters. Debris from several centuries of prehistoric culture has been found piled into mounds and middens in several places. One, Turtle Mound, rises 35 feet high. Visitors can climb to the top and get a sweeping view of ocean and bay waters.

Following Juan Ponce de Leon's visit to Florida in 1513, the Spanish explored the area bringing with them oranges, coconuts, pigs, and horses. None of the European explorers stayed long. Perhaps it was because of the heavy mosquito population around the lagoon where today, with the aid of insect repellent, people enjoy fishing, canoeing, and camping.

In 1830, the seeds of the nationally-known Indian River citrus industry were sown when Douglas Dummett established the first Florida citrus plantation on a spot just west of present-day State Route 3, about a mile north of Route 406. The citrus industry continues to be of commercial value to the area. Twelve citrus plantations operate within the seashore's boundaries under leasing agreements with the federal government.

In the late nineteenth century, people from the north began to push their way south to capitalize on Florida's sunny climate and burgeoning agricultural industry. In addition to the expansion of the railroad system that resulted, a water-borne route developed after a canal was built connecting Mosquito Lagoon and the Indian River. The community of Eldora sprang up on the east side of the lagoon to service the traffic. It was short-lived, however. The Intracoastal Waterway, established on the west side, became the major traffic route by the end of the century.

Canaveral National Seashore Today

Canaveral National Seashore is primarily a day-use park. There are no facilities for overnight stays and no concessions. But it has beautiful beaches; a fascinating variety of trees, plants, and wildlife that includes species indigenous to both northern and southern climes; great fishing and shellfishing; and a few historical sites.

After visiting such popular tourist attractions as the Kennedy Space Center, Disney World, and beach resorts, take a break and enjoy some quiet time. Loll on the beach, collect seashells, swim in the ocean, and drive or walk on quiet nature trails and search for alligators, eagles, pelicans, and wood storks. If you are prepared, fish in the ocean, canoe, or fish in the lagoon, or ride your horse on the beach. No matter what time of year you are in this part of Florida, you will enjoy a few hours spent at Canaveral National Seashore.

How To Get There

The seashore is within a short driving distance of major routes I-95 and U.S. 1. It lies within two counties. The northern half is in Volusia County; the southern half, adjacent to Kennedy Space Center, in Brevard County. Tourism and the aerospace industry dominate the economic life of the area.

You cannot drive directly from one end of the seashore to the other. To reach the northern end, take State Route 44 from I-95 to Florida A1A in the community of New Smyrna Beach. The seashore's northern boundary is six miles south.

To reach Canaveral's southern end, take Florida 406 from I-95 at Titusville. After crossing the Indian River, take Florida 402.

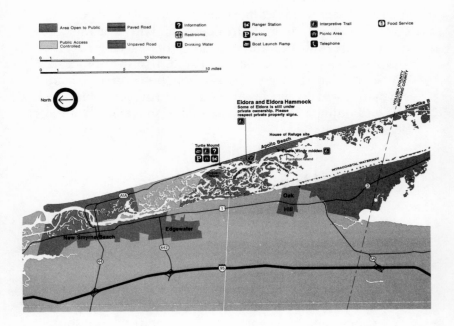

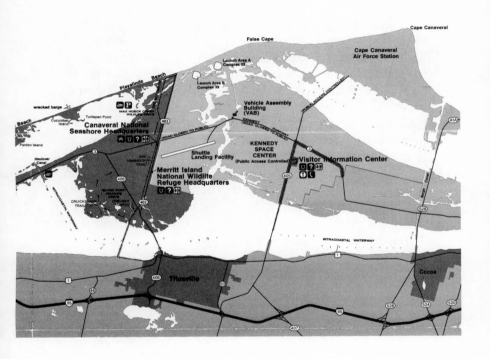

Where To Stay

Several major chains operate motels in the Titusville area. For information on these and other overnight accommodations, including campgrounds, in the Titusville area, contact the Titusville Chamber of Commerce. For information on New Smyrna Beach facilities, contact New Smyrna Beach-Edgewater Chamber of Commerce.

Camping No facilities are provided for camping. Primitive camping is permitted on Klondike Beach in fall, winter, and spring. Backcountry camping is permitted year round at sites on some of the islands in the northern part of Mosquito Lagoon, reachable only by boat. All equipment, including fresh water, must be brought with you and trash must be taken out. Be sure to take insect repellent and mosquito netting for the mosquitoes can be fierce, especially in summer.

To camp anywhere, obtain a free permit 24 hours in advance. For a map of sites and other information relating to camping, contact the information center or the seashore's Apollo Ranger Station on the beach road near Turtle Mound. Phone: 904/428–3384.

What To Do At Canaveral National Seashore

The Beaches There are two easily accessible beaches, Playalinda Beach at the south end and Apollo Beach at the north end, and a long stretch of beach in between. Parking places sufficient to accommodate 1,094 cars near Playalinda Beach and 175 cars near Apollo Beach, are located at frequent intervals behind the dune ridge. Parking is not permitted along the road.

Klondike Beach, which lies between the two, can only be reached by a good hike. For people who like isolated beaches, and enjoy a long beach walk and don't mind toting their own drinking water, this stretch of beach is inviting. Remember to wear a wide-brimmed sun-shielding hat.

Weekends and holidays in the spring and summer are the seashore's busiest seasons, so go to the beach early because when the parking spaces are full, the park is closed to further visitors.

There are no lifeguards at any of the beaches. However rangers, who are trained in surf rescue, patrol the beach regularly. Boardwalks must be used to cross from parking areas to the beach so that beach goers will not disturb dune vegetation which includes sand-holding sea oats, protected by state law.

The ocean waters are relatively warm, but swimmers should watch out for strong ocean currents and stinging jellyfish and the Portuguese man-of-war.

Surfboarding is popular. So is seashell collecting. A great array of shells, including coquina clam, lightning whelk, sand dollars, razor clam, angel wing, and moon shells can be found with little effort.

Playalinda Beach and other portions of the south end of the seashore are closed to the public for two days before the launching of a space vehicle and for a time preceding a landing at Kennedy Space Center. For detailed information on hours of closing and reopening, call Kennedy Space Center Information. Phone: 305/452–2121.

The Information Center Visitors to the north end of the seashore should stop at the information center a mile inside the park's entrance and see the exhibits and an audio-visual film. Rangers will provide information about ranger-led walks, canoe trips, Junior Ranger, and other programs and about all aspects of the seashore's resources. Such information can also be obtained at seashore headquarters at 2532 Garden Street, Titusville. The information center is open every day during daylight hours. Headquarters is open from 8 a.m. to 4 p.m. Monday through Friday.

To obtain information about the seashore before you go, call or write the Superintendent, Canaveral National Seashore.

The Merritt Island National Wildlife Refuge   If a sudden glimpse of a wild creature excites you and you instinctively lower your voice to a whisper, then you will enjoy a visit to Merritt Island National Wildlife Refuge.

Although the refuge is within the shadow of the sound and fury of space launches, its diverse resources continue to provide habitat for a tremendous variety of wildlife. Fresh, salt, and brackish water, pine flatwoods, and hardwood hammocks and an understory of both northern and southern plantlife attract more than 285 species of birds, 25 mammals, 117 fishes and 65 amphibians and reptiles. The refuge supports more wildlife on the Endangered or Threatened Species federal and state lists than any other refuge.

Wildlife can be seen throughout the area. Watch for gulls and terns, long-legged wading birds such as Great Blue Herons, Louisiana herons and snowy egrets, black skimmers, Roseate spoonbills, anhingas and, during the winter months, some of the 23 species of migrating wildfowl. Along the canal and waterways alligators quietly glide or sun themselves on rocks and banks. You may spot a Florida manatee or a bottle nose dolphin. Be sure to ask the rangers for tips on how to get to out-of-the-way places where some of the rarer wildlife are likely to be seen.

The headquarters of the Merritt Island National Wildlife Refuge is on State Route 402, about four miles after crossing the Indian River. It is open from 9 a.m. to 5 p.m., Monday through Saturday. Stop there and see the exhibits and get brochures about the refuge's inhabitants. Information may also be obtained by writing to Refuge Manager, Merritt Island National Wildlife Refuge.

The Trails Both the National Park Service (NPS) and the Fish and Wildlife Service (FWS) maintain driving and walking nature trails. The FWS Black Point Wildlife Drive through pine flatwoods and impounded marshes and Max Hoeck Creek Wildlife Drive through an impounded marsh offer excellent opportunities to see wildlife.

The entrance to Black Point Wildlife Drive is on State Route 406 running between Route 402 and Route 3. The tour is 7 miles long. As you enter, take a leaflet from a trailside box. It describes features to watch for at numbered stops. At stop #8, you can park your car and walk along a 5 mile foot trail. Or you can take a short walk to an observation tower. You may stop at any point on the drive to observe birds and animals or to examine methods used to control mosquitoes and provide habitat for wildlife at the same time.

The Max Hoeck Creek Wildlife Drive is a 5 mile auto tour beginning at Playalinda Beach. Here, too, the curious visitor is welcome to leave designated roads and walk any side road in search of wildlife.

While in the refuge area, you may want to walk the Oak Hammock Trail just beyond refuge headquarters, about 1.5 miles long. Interpretive signs identify the plants along the trail. Parking spaces are at the trailhead.

At the north end of the seashore there are several NPS self-guiding trails. At Turtle Mound, 200 yards north of the information center, you can take a short walk up over a pile of prehistoric shells and debris, now covered with trees and shrubs. A series of trailside plaques interpret the surroundings. Off-road parking is available.

Just beyond Turtle Mound, watch for the road to Eldora. Parking is available at Area #9 for people who want to walk a half-mile interpretive trail through a coastal hardwood hammock. About a mile down the road, another path through an oak hammock leads to a shell mound, Castle Windy midden, at the water's edge. Park at Area #3 and walk the .5 mile trail to the shores of the lagoon.

Rangers at the information center can direct you to other places to hike.

Horseback Riding   Horseback riding is permitted on the beach between parking area #13 at Playalinda Beach and The House of Refuge site and at Apollo Beach. To obtain a permit and further information, contact seashore headquarters or the Apollo Ranger Station at least 24 hours in advance of the time you want to ride. Ranger Station phone: 904/428-3384. Between May 15 and September 15, when endangered sea turtles nest on the beaches, horseback riding is not allowed.

Hunting, Fishing, And Boating   Waterfowl and other birds traversing the Atlantic Flyway have made the seashore area a stopping point for as long as man can remember and hunting in the marshes and lagoons has been a long-time practice. The season runs from about Thanksgiving to mid-January. For detailed information, contact either the seashore or refuge headquarters.

Both surf fishing and small boat fishing in the lagoon are popular sports. A Florida license is required for fresh water fishing. Shrimping, oystering, and clamming are widespread in the lagoon. Check Apollo Ranger Station for times oystering and clamming are permitted.

The Apollo Ranger Station can also provide a map showing a 2.5 mile self-guiding backcountry canoe trip. Two campsites are accessible from the canoe trail.

Boats can be launched at ramps at both ends of the seashore. For information on sites, check seashore headquarters or the information center. The Chamber of Commerce can provide information on boat rentals.

Oversand Vehicles (ORVs) No ORVs are permitted anywhere on the beaches of Canaveral National Seashore.

Pets Pets are not permitted on beaches. Elsewhere they must be on a leash no longer than 10 feet.

Historical/Cultural Resources Turtle Mound is listed on the National Register of Historic Places. Also listed are Old Haulover Canal, the Ross Hammock site which includes a midden and a burial mound, and the site of the Confederate Saltworks, all on the west side of the lagoon. Ask the rangers for directions to visit them.

Canaveral—The Atlantic's Final National Seashore

When traveling south from the northeast or mid-Atlantic regions, Canaveral National Seashore offers the beach lover the last chance to enjoy a federally-maintained stretch of natural beach on the Atlantic coast. No groins, no jetties, no docks, no fast-food places, no motels, no vendors; only sea, sand, lagoon, marshes, natural vegetation, and wildlife.

For Further Information, Contact:

Superintendent
Canaveral National Seashore
2532 Garden St.
Titusville, FL 32796
Phone: 407/267–1110

Manager
Merritt Island National Wildlife Refuge
P.O. Box 6504
State Road 402
Titusville, FL 32782
Phone: 407/867–0667

Titusville Chamber of Commerce
2000 S. Washington Ave.
Titusville, FL 32780
Phone: 407/267–3036

New Smyrna Beach-Edgewater
Oak Hill Chamber of Commerce
115 Canal St.
New Smyrna Beach, FL 32168
Phone: 1/800/541–9621
904/428–2449

Gulf Islands National Seashore

For want of grass the sand is lost, for want of sand the dune is lost, for want of the dune, the island is lost, for want of the island the harbor is lost.

This inscription on a plaque alongside the boardwalk leading from the dock to the beach at West Ship Island, Mississippi District of the Gulf Islands National Seashore, says it all. No "Stay Off the Grass" sign could so effectively alert the seashore visitor to the sensitive inter-relationship of maritime resources. Sea oats, the tall, slim, golden-tasseled grass that abounds on the Gulf Islands, tolerate salt spray and catch the sand, their long spreading root system holding the dunes in place against the winds.

Sea oats once were harvested and sold to florists on the mainland. Alarmed by the detrimental effect sea oats picking had on the beach environment, laws were passed to protect them. In Florida fines up to $500.00 can be imposed on anyone who picks sea oats.

The Gulf Islands National Seashore includes all or parts of six barrier islands, two in Florida and four in Mississippi, that skip across a 150-mile stretch of startling azure Gulf of Mexico waters. The seashore offers over 100 miles of magnificent beaches composed of fine sand so white it looks like new-fallen snow. It also includes the well-cared-for remains of four nineteenth century masonry forts built to protect the southern flank of a young nation and numerous late nineteenth and early twentieth century concrete forts. There is also a rare historical preserve of live oak hammocks, and the only Southern bayou within a national seashore.

Dynamic coastal processes are constantly reshaping the Gulf Islands. Wind and wave action push the sands from east to west, and overwash and inlet formation change the landscape. Dunes are flattened; then subsequent gentle breezes rebuild them. Little effort is made to stabilize the beaches on seashore property.

The islands lie in the path of severe storms and hurricanes generated in the Gulf of Mexico and the Caribbean Sea. Damaging hurricanes have occurred on the average of once every ten years. In recent times, small islands have disappeared and in 1969, a "100 year" storm, Hurricane Camille, made two islands out of one.

The Gulf Islands Before The National Seashore

The French were there. The Spanish were there. So were the British. And before them, Indians inhabited the lands embraced by the waters of the Gulf Islands. In 1803 the United States acquired the Mississippi lands as part of the Louisiana Purchase, and in 1821 western Florida officially became part of the fast-growing country when a treaty with Spain was ratified.

Soon after, additions to an expanding national coastal defense system were designed to protect strategic Gulf coast waters. Fort Pickens on the western tip of Santa Rosa Island (built between 1829 and 1834) and Fort McRee on the eastern edge of Perdido Key (built between 1835-1839) guarded the entrance to Pensacola Bay. High on a bluff on a peninsula overlooking the Bay, the site of an old Spanish fortification became the locale of Fort Barrancas (completed in 1844). One-half mile to the north of the fort, the Advanced Redoubt (outpost) was built to defend the peninsula on which the U.S. Navy Yard was located.

Across the waters to the west, off the coast of Mississippi, Ship Island[1] was made a U.S. military reservation in 1847. Key to the defense of New Orleans, U.S. Army engineers constructed a fort on this island to protect the gateway to the Mississippi River Delta.

[1] The English version of the French appelation "Isle aux Vaisseaux," so named by an early French explorer because of the island's protected deep-water anchorage for his ships.

The Gulf Islands And The Civil War

The fort on Ship Island was far from being completed when the Civil War erupted in early 1861. Confederate troops occupied the island for several months. At one time the fort exchanged cannon fire with the Union Ship *Massachusetts*. After the Confederate forces abandoned the island, it became an active Union military site. Hastily constructed wooden buildings were used for hospitals, barracks, and a prisoner-of-war camp. A U.S. military prison stockade, in use from 1862 to 1870, housed thousands of military convicts during its time.

In Florida, the Confederacy controlled all the coastal military installations but Fort Pickens. By May 1862, however, the troops were needed elsewhere and they pulled out, whereupon Union forces reoccupied all the Pensacola area fortifications.

By the late nineteenth century, advances in weaponry made the masonry fortification coastal defense system obsolete. And by the end of World War II techniques of warfare were so changed that it was no longer necessary to reserve so much coastal land for national defense.

The offshore islands of the Gulf were not only of military importance; they were a key factor in the culture and economics of the region. Deep water harbors made them an ideal initial landing point for Europeans destined for lands bordering the Gulf coast. Throughout the nineteenth century, ocean-going vessels unloaded their passengers on these islands, from which they were transported in lighter vessels to the mainland.

A lighthouse was built on Ship Island in 1852 and rebuilt in 1886. The island was a busy lumber port when sail-powered vessels were the prime means of shipping timber.

The nation's first quarantine station for yellow fever victims was built on the east end of Ship Island in 1880.

In time, commercial fishing and recreational pursuits eclipsed all other activities in and around the island.

The Making Of The Gulf Islands National Seashore

Nowhere in the southern region were there so many beautifully formed beaches gently sloping into the clear waters of the Gulf as along the western Florida barrier islands. In the years after World War II these long stretches of open land, no longer needed by the military, invited development of one sort or another. State and local governments picked out island and coastal sites to turn into parks for the enjoyment of their citizens. Private developers touted nearby choice lots for vacation retreats. A university acquired a coastal site for recreation and possible research purposes. Various agencies of the federal government found large tracts of land useful for their own purposes, including the establishment of two wildlife refuges.

Gulf coast residents expressed concern about the potential effect of development of Mississippi's offshore islands on the abundant bird life that had for centuries found protection in the isolation of islands 10 or 12 miles off the coast. Local history buffs worried lest the periodically harsh weather destroy revered historical and cultural sites. Interest in preservation began to take hold.

A group of Mississippi citizens, appalled at the waters lapping at the base of the fort, now known as Fort Massachusetts, on Ship Island, decided to take action. They formed a group, "Save the Fort," in 1965 and raised $23,000.00 in private donations. A large part of the money was never used because so many people donated time, materials, and services, ferrying rocks across 12 miles of bay waters and shoring up the base of the fort as a temporary measure until a more permanent arrangement could be made. The movement was termed "a labor of love."

The group appealed to the city, the county, then the state, with no success. Then they heard about a group of

Florida citizens who were trying to save the forts of the Pensacola area. They joined forces, took advantage of the current federal interest in expanding federal recreation areas, and by the early 1970s, they had a winning proposition: a national seashore for the northeastern Gulf coast that would include a number of existing beaches suitable for high density use, some remote natural islands that would remain largely untouched, and several historical sites - something for everyone. The Gulf Islands National Seashore was authorized by law on January 8, 1971.

Gulf Islands National Seashore Today

Gulf Islands National Seashore is the largest of the seashores. Its boundaries encompass more acreage than any other seashore. It has the greatest number of visitors, over 7.5 million in 1986. Its temperate climate draws people year-round. With districts both in Florida and Mississippi (separated by the state of Alabama), Gulf Islands seems almost to be two seashores. Each has its distinct recreational appeal.

The National seashore is headquartered in Gulf Breeze, Florida just south of Pensacola in the western panhandle of the state. All Florida facilities–beaches, forts, and the Naval Live Oaks Area–are easily reached accross well-traveled roads. In 1988, over three million people came to or drove through the Florida District. Some were local residents who traverse seashore roads in the course of their daily lives.

The Mississippi District has a mainland base at Ocean Springs, 4 miles from Biloxi. Its unique character lies in its four mostly undeveloped offshore islands, reachable only by an hour-long trip across the Mississippi Sound in a private or concession boat. The Mississippi District hosted over a million visitors in 1988.

The Florida District

How To Get There

The several units of the Florida District are spread out over a wide area in the vicinity of Pensacola. Interstate

Route 10, a major east-west route in the southeastern portion of the country, borders the northern edge of Pensacola.

Where To Stay

Private Accommodations Pensacola and Pensacola Beach are replete with hotels and motels. For information contact major hotel/motel chains or the Pensacola Area Chamber of Commerce, Visitor Information Center.

Camping Information on camping at state parks and private campgrounds can be obtained from the Pensacola Area Chamber of Commerce.

What To Do At The Florida District

Where you start your visit depends on what you want to do first - visit historic fortifications, the beaches or the Naval Live Oaks Area.

Fort Barrancas

To visit Fort Barrancas and its related fortifications, take Florida Route 295 through the main entrance to the Pensacola Naval Air Station; then following directions to the fort. Rangers at the Fort Barrancas Visitor Information Station will give you a pamphlet about the fort and answer questions. The building has facilities for handicapped visitors. There are guided tours daily all year long. The fort is open from 9:30 a.m. to 5 p.m. in season; in the winter, from 10:30 a.m. to 4 p.m. While at the Naval Air Station, you may also want to visit the nearby Naval Aviation Museum.

Naval Live Oaks Area

A new visitor center featuring exhibits and audio-visual programs will open at the Naval Live Oaks Area in 1988. The building will serve as the seashore administrative headquarters. Nearby there are picnic facilities, a half-mile nature trail, and restrooms.

The Naval Live Oaks Area is of special significance to the conservation-minded visitor. In the early days of the country, live oaks were cut down extensively for use in building naval vessels. But in 1828 President John Quincy Adams inaugurated the first federal timber conservation program by setting aside a large stand of live oak trees for federal protection and this land is part of the original reservation.

To reach the Naval Live Oaks Area from Pensacola, take the Pensacola Bay Bridge, U.S. Route 98, to Gulf Breeze, then continue on U.S. 98 east a short distance to the marked site.

Fort Pickens And The Beaches

A short toll bridge from Gulf Breeze, crossing Santa Rosa Sound, will take you to Santa Rosa Island and highly developed Pensacola Beach. Turn to the west and drive along Fort Pickens Road for 3 miles to the entrance to the seashore's Fort Pickens site. A $3.00 per car or a $1.00 per person entrance fee, good for a seven day period, will be collected. Persons planning frequent visits may purchase a $10.00 annual permit. Holders of "Golden" passports are excepted.

About 5 miles west of the entrance station, you will come to Langdon Beach with a 100-car parking lot, snack shop, showers, picnic tables, and lifeguards in season. Beyond Langdon Beach there are signs to a bike trail, the Dune Nature Trail, additional picnic sites, several late nineteenth and early twentieth century concrete batteries, some with guns in place and a fishing pier.

A visitor information station is located near Fort Pickens, the brick fort. Visitors can view exhibits, buy books and pamphlets, and get the schedule of ranger-conducted programs, including fort tours, snorkeling, and sea life programs. A snack bar is available. Most buildings are open 9:30 a.m. to 5 p.m.; in winter, 10:30 a.m. to 4 p.m.

There are several other seashore beaches besides the one at the Fort Pickens area. Ten miles east of Pensacola Beach is the Santa Rosa Area beach. Restrooms, picnic areas, and an exhibit room are open year-round. Bathhouses and concessions are open in the spring and summer. The beach is lifeguarded in the summer. All facilities are accessible to disabled visitors.

Twenty six miles east of the Santa Rosa facility, past Eglin Air Force Base and Fort Walton Beach, is another national seashore beach, Okaloosa Area. It is on the Choctawhatchee Bay. It has restrooms, outdoor showers, a picnic area, and concessions (spring & summer).

Johnson Beach at the Perdido Key Area is equipped with lifeguards from Memorial Day to Labor Day and has showers, picnic areas, and concessions. To get there, travel southwest of Pensacola on Florida Route 292 which leads into Florida Route 293, taking you across to the Key. A left turn at the first fork in the road soon places you at the beach. Fort McRee, built on the tip of Perdido Key as part of the Pensacola coastal defense system, no longer exists. Its remains are now under water. However, visitors interested in viewing remnants of the island's early coastal defenses may want to take a 6 mile hike to the end of Per-

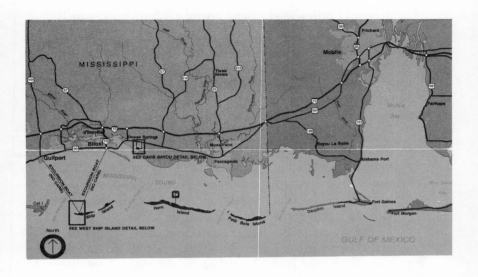

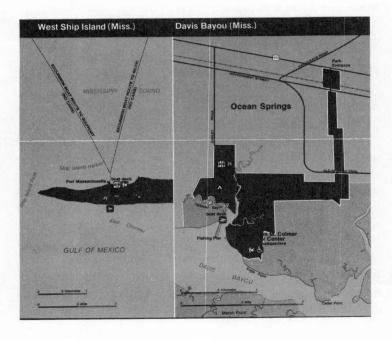

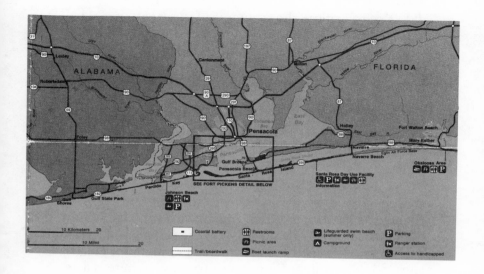

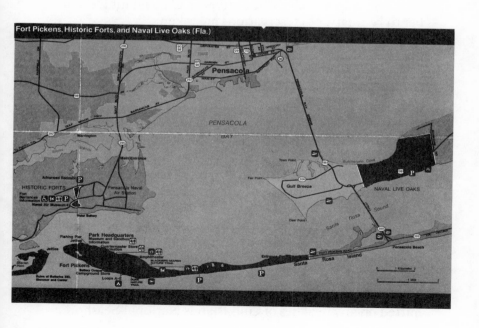

dido Key to explore the remnants of three batteries, identified as Batteries Slemmer, Center, and 233 (1898-1942).

The beaches of Gulf Island's Florida District are extremely popular in the summertime. Many parking spaces
are spotted throughout the area but sometimes the lots are
full and it is necessary to park along the road. Use
boardwalks, when available, to get to the beach so that you
will not trample the beach grasses which hold the sand in
place.

Camping   Camping is especially appealing at Fort
Pickens. It is the only seashore camping unit on a barrier
island that has a forest environment with vehicle camping
not far from the beach. At the 200-site campground, open
year-round, the 1987 fee was $10.00 per night for electric
sites, $8.00 per night for non-electric sites. There is a 14-
day limit from March to November, a 30-day limit December to February. No reservations are taken.

Group tent camping, for which reservations must be
made, is available at Fort Pickens Area and at a youth camp
site at the Naval Live Oaks Area. For information, contact
Campground Registration, Gulf Islands National
Seashore.

Food and other supplies, and laundry facilities can be
found at the campground store at the Fort Pickens site.

Fishing And Hunting   No license is required for
salt water fishing along seashore beaches.

Hunting is allowed on the Santa Rosa sound side of
the Santa Rosa Area and the Big Lagoon side of Perdido
Key Area during the Florida season for dove, ducks, and
geese. Federal and state regulations apply.

Oversand Vehicles (ORVs)   ORVs are not permitted on any beaches of Gulf Islands National Seashore.

Pets You may bring pets to Gulf Islands National Seashore but they must be kept on a leash. You may not take them into any public buildings or structures or on the beaches.

SCUBA Diving SCUBA diving is permitted at seashore beaches but check with a ranger for recommended sites and regulations.

The Mississippi District

For anyone who wants to take the time to gain a real understanding of the interdependence of a barrier island, the coastal mainland it protects, and life in the waters between, there is no better place than the Mississippi District of the Gulf Islands National Seashore. Go there for a vivid, "hands on" experience of the special life processes within the nutrient-rich waters of the bayou, the bay, and the barrier island.

How To Get There

Mississippi District headquarters is at Davis Bayou, Ocean Springs. Ocean Springs is on U.S. Route 90 which runs through almost all the coastal communities of Mississippi. From U.S. 90, there is a clearly-marked "Park entrance" road which runs 3 miles south to the attractive visitor center. The visitor center is open 9 a.m. to 6 p.m. in summer; 8 a.m. to 5 p.m. the rest of the year.

Where To Stay

Private Accommodations For information, contact major hotel/motel chains or the Mississippi Gulf Coast Convention and Visitors Bureau.

Camping For information on state and private campgrounds, contact the Mississippi Gulf Coast Convention and Visitors Bureau.

What To Do At The Mississippi District

There are many things to do at the Mississippi District, both at the mainland site and on the off shore islands. First, enjoy the exhibits at the visitor center featuring paintings by a local artist who spent much of his life camping, studying, painting and sketching the plants and animals on the off shore islands. Be sure to see the excellent film depicting the flora, fauna, and life processes of the beach, bay, and marshland. Take a self-guided nature walk or fish from the pier. In the summer, take a ranger-conducted boat trip through the quiet waters of the bayou, and absorb the sights and sounds of the creatures that thrive in a salt marsh.

If you are there between April 1 and September 30, take time to visit one or more of the seashore's off shore islands. Staff at the mainland visitor center can provide schedule and fee information about concession boat trips from Gulfport or Biloxi to West Ship Island. Charter boat service is available to East Ship Island (split off from the western end of Ship Island by a 1969 storm), Horn Island, and Petit Bois Island. Reservations are necessary. For information, write Gulf Islands National Seashore.

The Beaches There is no sandy beach on the mainland, but the off shore islands offer fine, primitive beaches. To get to the park-maintained beach on West Ship Island, take the hour-long boat trip across Mississippi Sound. (The bay is so shallow that a "Biloxi Schooner" was specially designed for commercial use.) Once on the island you can swim, sunbathe, or gather shells on a beautiful beach facing the Gulf. In summer, the beach has lifeguards, bath houses, a snack bar, and covered picnic tables.

Visit the Guard Room at Fort Massachusetts to learn the history of the fort and buy publications about the area's resources and cultural history.

Camping Davis Bayou campground, nestled among the towering trees of a former state park, provides 51 modern camping sites, each with water. There are showers, restrooms, and a dump station. The 1987 campsite fee was $10.00 per electric site, and $8.00 per non-electric site per night. No reservations are taken. There is a 14-day limit from January through March; a 30 day limit April through December.

Tent camping for groups may be arranged through advance registration. Write the Gulf Islands National Seashore. A public boat ramp, ball field, and picnic shelters are at nearby sites.

Primitive camping is allowed on East Ship, Horn, and Petit Bois Islands year round. Campers must bring their food and water.

No lifeguards are available at the beaches. Be prepared to cope with insects in warm months! Take plenty of repellent and netting. Horn and Petit Bois Islands have been designated "wilderness areas."

You may see nesting osprey, ducks, and geese in winter, the rare frigate bird in summer. You may also come upon trash, surely out of keeping with a wilderness island. It is constantly being washed in from the sea. No mechanized vehicles or equipment may be used in a wilderness area, so the trash remains. But do not compound the problem. Take out what you bring to the island so that your "imprint" will be gone after you've enjoyed the rare opportunity to be immersed in a natural seashore environment.

Endangered Species   If you are alert, you may spot some of the endangered wildlife species that inhabit the offshore islands. They include brown pelican, Arctic peregrine falcon, American alligator, leatherback turtle, Atlantic Ridley turtle, and Southern Bald Eagle.

Fishing And Hunting   No license is required for salt water fishing. Hunting is not allowed.

Pets   Similar rules apply as in the Florida District. Pets are not allowed on the concession boats from Biloxi and Gulfport to West Ship Island. If you go by private boat to East Ship, Horn, or Petit Bois Islands, you may take pets, but they must be on leashes while on the islands.

Historical/Cultural Resources   This seashore is replete with historical evidence. Indian middens have been discovered. Shipwrecks lie in the deep waters of the Gulf. The National Register of Historic Places includes the Fort Massachusetts Historic District on Ship Island, the Fort Pickens Historic District on Santa Rosa Island, Fort Barrancas Historic District within the Pensacola Naval Air Station and Perdido Key Historic District on Perdido Key. Other places such as the lighthouse on Ship Island and the Naval Live Oaks District have been nominated.

The Gulf Islands National Seashore—A Year-Round Attraction

Gulf Islands National Seashore will undoubtedly continue to be heavily used. Most visitors come from Mississippi, Louisiana, Alabama, Florida, and adjacent southern states. At times, particularly around Easter and the summer holidays, the Florida beaches are heavily used, and on some summer weekends the boats to West Ship Island are full.

Summer isn't the only time the seashore appeals to the vacationer, however. Non-beach activity such as camping, nature trail hiking, bird watching, and visiting historic sites are delightful pursuits in fall, winter, and early spring when the temperature is more comfortable, insects are scarce, and there are no crowds. Many Midwesterners already enjoy winter vacations there. As Americans continue to increase their mobility, people from the North and Far West, searching for new, appealing destinations, will undoubtedly discover this seashore's year-round attractions and head for the Gulf Islands.

For More Information, Contact:

Superintendent
Florida District
Gulf Islands National Seashore
1801 Gulf Breeze Parkway
Gulf Breeze, FL 32561
Phone: 904/934–2600

Campground Registration
Gulf Islands National Seashore
1801 Gulf Breeze Parkway
Gulf Breeze, FL 32561
Phone: 904/932–5018

Superintendent
Gulf Islands National Seashore
Mississippi District
3500 Park Road
Ocean Springs, MS 39564
Phone: 601/875–0821
(Campground Registration, phone: 601/875–3962)

Pensacola Area Chamber of Commerce
Visitor Information Center
1401 East Gregory St.
Pensacola, FL 32501
Phone: in Florida 1/800/343–4321
elsewhere: 1/800/874–1234

Mississippi Gulf Coast Convention and Visitors Bureau
P.O. Box 6128
Gulfport, MS 39506
Phone: 1/800/237–9493
601/896–6699

Padre Island National Seashore

"Her treasure is the gold of her sun, the silver of her moonlight, and the sapphire of her pearl-crusted waves. This treasure requires no iron strong box. It is safe from the greedy hands of man. . . I dedicate it with the hope that we — as its stewards — will be worthy of the trust."

From a 1766 survey report quoted by Mrs. Lyndon B. Johnson in remarks at the dedication of Padre Island National Seashore April 8, 1968.

T he devoted explorer of undeveloped coastal beaches should travel to southeast Texas beyond Corpus Christi to Padre Island National Seashore on the Gulf of Mexico. This seashore offers almost 70 miles of mostly undeveloped shore on the largest barrier island in the United States.

A first-time visitor may be astonished at the sight. As the drive begins down the park road in the center of the island, in full view are all the features of a dynamic barrier island: vegetated stabilized dunes, wide stretches of grasslands, a sandy beach gently sloping into Gulf waters, actively moving "blowout" dunes, ponds where rain waters have filled wind-scoured troughs, fertile tidal flats, and a blue lagoon between the island and the mainland.

There is space on Padre Island—wide open expanses to view, photograph, walk on, or drive along. Until 1987, a portion of the beach was set aside for those who prefer to swim, sunbathe, collect shells, and picnic with lifeguard service, showers, restrooms, and food concessions at hand. However, the erosional effects of salt and sea water caused severe structural damage to the visitor pavilion around which these activities focused and, temporarily, this section of beach is closed and these services have been suspended until a new facility can be built.

Beach lovers who enjoy a primitive setting, however, will be in their element at Padre Island National Seashore. The beach extends for miles and miles and, if you are prepared to hike a considerable distance or travel in an appropriate vehicle, you can find vast, empty stretches of sand.

Padre Island stretches 113 miles along the curving southern Texas coastline, reaching almost to the Mexican border. Only Brazos Island, across Brazos Santiago Pass, separates it. On the north, Padre Island is joined to Mustang Island. Corpus Christi Pass once divided the islands but the opening is now filled.

A man-made passage from lagoon to Gulf, called Mansfield Channel, intersects the island about three-quarters of the way to its natural southern border. The seashore's boundaries end at the channel. The island varies in width from a few hundred yards to about three miles.

A portion of Laguna Madre, through which the Intracoastal Waterway passes, forms the western border of the seashore. The seashore's boundaries encompass several islands in the lagoon that are important bird nesting sites.

Padre Island is a young barrier island. It was formed by the joining of many smaller islands less than 3,000 years

ago and it is continually changing. Strong and steady blowing winds, the converging off shore of strong ocean currents
coming from different directions, and great tides, storms,
and hurricanes constantly alter the landscape. Padre Island
is truly a place where a person can observe "Nature in the
raw."

The "stewards" of the island, the National Park Service, acknowledge the island's natural, fast-moving evolu-
tionary process. Only minimal facilities to service visitors
have been built at the north end of the seashore (now in
the process of being rebuilt). Visitors are urged to join in
conserving the island's resources. But the seashore management faces a formidable challenge from a strange mix of
natural and human actions beyond its control.

A map of Padre Island graphically illustrates the
problem. The island bends westward, curving from the
northeast to the southeast. Wind directions vary seasonal-
ly. In the winter, winds generally blow from the northeast.
Ocean currents, streaming with the wind, push approaching Gulf waters in a southerly direction. In the summer, impelled by winds from the southeast, the currents move
northward. There are times when these currents meet off
shore of the middle of the island's curvature—usually in
spring and late fall. The meeting ground is known as the
zone of convergence. At this point the sea flowing across
the Gulf of Mexico pushes any object in its path directly
on to the shore of Padre Island.

Many things, both natural and man-made, exist, fall,
or are dumped into the Gulf of Mexico: tropical sea beans
from far-away shores, various shells and other forms of
marine life, tar seeping from the floor of the Gulf. And such
products of modern society as oil from spills or tanker flush-
ings, plastic sheets, and drums of hazardous waste. To clean
up and haul away this unending debris from the seashore's
beaches on a daily basis is a mammoth, extremely costly,

undertaking. Consequently, in the past when the seashore maintained a small section of developed beach area, that was the only place regularly swept. Arrangements are made to have the potentially dangerous washed-up drums removed from the shore. The rest remains until scavengers carry it away or high tides pull it back into the sea.

Padre Island Before The National Seashore

Blowing sands and violent storm waters have erased most of the traces of Padre Island's earliest inhabitants, the Karankawa Indians. It is known from reports of early European visitors that the Indians summered on the island, fished in the lagoon, hunted on the mainland, and gathered fruits and nuts. When the Europeans came, the natives refused to abandon their culture, bitterly fighting to the end. They no longer exist.

Isla Blanca, the White Island, is what Alonso de Peñeda called the island when he was exploring and charting the north and west coasts of the Gulf of Mexico on behalf of the Spanish governor of Jamaica in 1519. The Spanish were the dominant European presence in the southwest for the next two hundred and fifty years. They chose not to make their homes on Padre Island but mainland ranchers grazed cattle there.

In 1800, Padre Nicolas Ballí, for whom the island is now named, received a grant to the island from the King of Spain. With the help of his nephew, Juan José Ballí, he set up an extensive ranching operation based at his Santa Cruz Ranch. For over 170 years, at different times under Spanish, Mexican, Texan, or United States government authority, ranching was the predominant economic venture on the island. Grazing ended in the national seashore in 1971.

The Making Of The Padre Island National Seashore

The first move to entice tourists to Padre Island is generally credited to a real estate developer, Colonel Sam Robertson. He bought some of the holdings of Patrick Dunn, the island's last major cattle rancher, and built a wooden causeway to the island from Corpus Christi in 1927. He provided ferry service to both ends of the island and built a hotel.

But the 1929 depression and a 1933 hurricane that destroyed the bridge and some buildings on the island stopped the tourist boom before it got started. Others who saw Padre Island as a potential vacation spot formed the Padre Island Park Association in the late 1930s and started a campaign to establish a state park there. Litigation over land ownership and World War II delayed action.

Causeways were built from Corpus Christi and from Port Isabel in the early 1950s. With easy access to both north and south ends of Padre Island then available, the way was paved for large-scale resort development.

But local citizens interested in preserving Padre Island took note of a widely circulated National Park Service report that revealed a scarcity in the nation's public seashore recreation areas and cited Padre Island as a beach that should be placed in public ownership. With the support of the area's congressional delegation and a leading newspaper, they mounted a drive to establish a national seashore on Padre Island.

Their efforts paralleled those working to get a national seashore at Cape Cod, Massachusetts and at Point Reyes, California. Senator Ralph Yarborough introduced the first bill and on September 28, 1962, barely a year after Cape Cod and fifteen days after Point Reyes National Seashores were established, President John F. Kennedy signed the law authorizing a national seashore on Padre Island.

Padre Island National Seashore Today

Padre Island National Seashore is primarily a place to relax and enjoy swimming, sunbathing, beachcombing, and fishing. It is also a place where those so inclined can study beach ecology, search for marine life, watch birdlife, or sail or motor in the shallow waters of the lagoon.

The seashore is most popular with local and regional visitors during the long, hot summer when persons living in the subtropical climate of South Texas seek relief in the waters and breezes of the Gulf. Winters are short. At times very cold winds, called "northers" sweep across the island causing a sudden drop in temperature, high surf, and very choppy waters in the lagoon. When storms are expected in winter or in hurricane season, normally August through October, seashore rangers alert campers and other visitors. The seashore offers daily recorded messages regarding weather, tides, shelling, beach conditions, and fishing. Phone: 512/949–8175.

Out-of-state visitors tend to frequent the seashore in fall, winter, and spring. Many come in recreational vehicles and stay several days to enjoy the pleasant coastal weather.

The out-of-towner's first stop should be at the temporary Malaquite Visitor Center. There are exhibits relating to the seashore's resources and publications for sale. Rangers will give you tips about beachcombing and driving on the beach and information about seashells, the island's 350 species of birds and native fish, mammals, and plants. In summer, rangers conduct interpretive walks and demonstrations.

How To Get There

The most direct route to Padre Island National Seashore is by way of Corpus Christi. Corpus Christi is 145 miles southeast of San Antonio via U.S. I-37. Coming from Houston, go southwest on U.S. Route 59 to U.S. Route 77. Route 77 joins U.S. I-37 on the outskirts of Corpus Christi. Approximately 11 miles within the city limits, take State Route 358, South Padre Island Drive, which leads directly to Park Road 22 crossing Kennedy Causeway over Laguna Madre. Drive south from the causeway approximately 12 miles to the entrance to the seashore.

An entrance fee of $1.00 per person (maximum $3.00 per vehicle) will be collected with $10.00 annual permits also available. Holders of Golden Passports do not pay an entrance fee.

Before you cross the causeway you may want to stop at seashore headquarters in Corpus Christi to get a park brochure and other free handouts telling you about "things to see and do" and park resources. The office is located at 9405 South Padre Island Drive in the Flour Bluff area, 21 miles from the park's entrance. It is open weekdays from 8 a.m. to 4:30 p.m. This material is also available on the island at the temporary visitor center in the parking lot at the site of the former Malaquite (pronounced Mal-a-keet) Pavilion. The visitor center is open daily from 9 a.m. to 4 p.m., and until 6 p.m. in summer.

Though the seashore extends for 68.5 miles, you can drive a conventional vehicle, trailer, or recreational vehicle on park property for only 13.5 miles. The first 8.5 miles is on hard-surfaced road, the last 5 miles on the beach. Driving on the wet, hard-packed, fine sand characteristic of this section of the beach apparently does little or no harm to the seashore's resources.

Caution is advised. No facilities for gas or tow service exist. Speed limits are posted and the beach is patrolled.

Watch out especially for two things: persons walking, playing, or lying on the beach who may not hear an approaching car because of the sound of the surf, and piles of flotsam and jetsam washing in from the sea. The latter may well include a Portuguese man-of-war or "blue jellyfish" which sends out poisonous and painful little darts when disturbed, whether the creature is alive or dead. Persons with arms resting on a car windowsill have been known to feel the sting!

Beyond this point, the texture of the beach changes. Great quantities of shells are mixed with the fine sand, forming a rough, ridged surface. Only four-wheel "street legal" vehicles may be driven for the remaining 50 miles to the Mansfield Channel.

See section on ORVs for further information.

Where To Stay

Except for a limited number of campsites, no overnight facilities are provided within the seashore. When the boundaries of the seashore were set, land on both the north and south ends of the island was specifically excluded so that commercial facilities could be located in those areas and the park could remain in its natural state.

Private Accommodations Several major motel chains operate motels in Corpus Christi and at South Padre Island, a popular resort area south of Mansfield Channel. (There is no bridge across the channel.) A few motels, along with a wide assortment of condominiums that offer daily and weekly rentals, restaurants, and convenience stores are also available in Port Aransas, a friendly, tourist-oriented, waterfront community at the northern tip of Mustang Island.

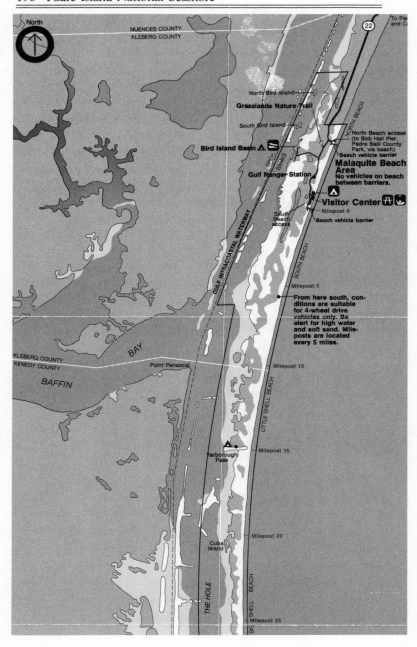

North

NUECES COUNTY
KLEBERG COUNTY

To Por
and C

22

North Bird Island

Grasslands Nature Trail

South Bird Island

Bird Island Basin

Gulf Ranger Station

SPOIL BANKS

NORTH BEACH

North Beach access
(to Bob Hall Pier,
Padre Balli County
Park, via beach)

Beach vehicle barrier

Malaquite Beach
Area
No vehicles on beach
between barriers.

Visitor Center

Milepost 0

Beach vehicle barrier

South
Beach
access

GULF INTRACOASTAL WATERWAY

SOUTH BEACH

Milepost 5

From here south, con-
ditions are suitable
for 4-wheel drive
vehicles only. Be
alert for high water
and soft sand. Mile-
posts are located
every 5 miles.

KLEBERG COUNTY
KENEDY COUNTY

BAY

Point Penascal

Milepost 10

BAFFIN

LITTLE SHELL BEACH

Milepost 15

Yarborough
Pass

Milepost 20

Cuba
Island

THE HOLE

BIG SHELL BEACH

Milepost 25

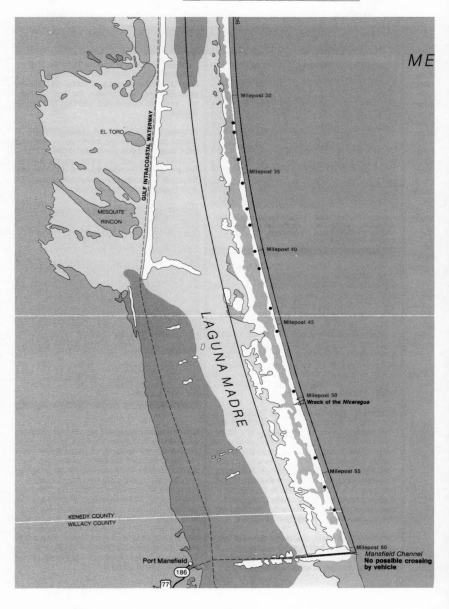

0 1 Kilometer 5   10
0 1 Mile   5   10

ME

Milepost 30

EL TORO

GULF INTRACOASTAL WATERWAY

Milepost 35

MESQUITE
RINCON

Milepost 40

LAGUNA MADRE

Milepost 45

Milepost 50
△ Wreck of the *Nicaragua*

Milepost 55

KENEDY COUNTY
WILLACY COUNTY

Milepost 60
Mansfield Channel
**No possible crossing
by vehicle**

Port Mansfield
(186)
To (77)

For motel information, check directories of major motel chains or call their free "800" numbers, or write to Corpus Christi Convention and Tourist Bureau. The Port Aransas Area Chamber of Commerce, Tourist and Convention Bureau, can provide information and accommodations in that community.

For information on accommodations on Padre Island south of the seashore, write South Padre Island Tourist Bureau.

Camping   Three types of camping are permitted: in designated park-maintained campsites located on the Gulf side of the island, in primitive camping areas at Bird Island Basin and Yarborough Pass on the lagoon, and on the beach. No reservations are accepted.

The park campground, located near the temporary visitor center, has 41 campsites. Facilities include fresh water, cold showers, restrooms, a dump station, and picnic tables. A modest fee is charged. No electrical hookups are available.

Chemical toilets and picnic tables are provided at the primitive sites at the Bird Island Basin location and at campsites at Yarborough Pass. Chemical toilets are also provided at intervals on the beach.

North of the park, camping is available at Neuces County Padre Balli Park and at Mustang Island State Park. The county park has a laundry, hot showers, and a dump station. For information on fees and regulations, write to the park. Mustang Island State Park also has hot showers plus hookups. For further details, write Mustang Island State Park. Cameron County provides campsites, a trailer park with hook-ups, and 17 motel units at South Padre Island. For information write Cameron County Park.

What To Do At Padre Island

The Beaches Surfboarding is permitted except within the restricted Malaquite beach area. Because of its shallow waters, the seashore's beaches are not considered good for SCUBA diving. Swimmers are cautioned about strong rip currents and about sudden drop-offs in the beach's waters due to underwater sand bars.

No vehicles of any sort are permitted in front of the pavilion at Malaquite Beach. Neither is surf fishing allowed in this area.

Many people choose to set up a base for their activities further down the beach. For as far as two-wheel drive vehicles (conventional cars) may be driven, cars are parked, blankets are spread out, and tents are erected. Where conventional car driving ends, Little Shell Beach begins. This beach, so named for shells of small clams brought to this point by longshore currents from the north, extends for approximately 10 miles.

At Yarborough Pass, marked only by a primitive road through the dunes to the other side of the island, Little Shell Beach merges with Big Shell Beach. Shells of larger clams from the south have been deposited there by northerly flowing currents. The terrain changes at Big Shell Beach. The beach is steeper and the dunes are higher.

Toward the southern end of the seashore past Big Shell Beach, the beach levels out and the dune line begins to diminish and eventually disappears. Actively migrating dunes and scarce vegetation characterize the landward side of the beach.

If you like to beachcomb, keep an eye out for ghost crabs scurrying in the sand, mole clams, and other sea creatures. You can also collect sea beans, shells such as Lightning whelks, Scotch bonnets, sand dollars, and Sea Whip, a curious soft coral formed into yellow or red wiry strands. Wear old footgear because just under the surface of the sand are patches of tar. The tar will cling to anything that touches it and it is very difficult to remove.

If you should see a 30 or 55 gallon drum washed up on the beach, do not go near it. It may contain a hazardous substance. Report its location to the first seashore staff person you meet.

If you plan to hike or drive a great distance on the beach it is wise to check first with a ranger to find out about beach conditions and get advice on how to prepare for any contingency. Call the Ranger Station, 512/949–8173, or the visitor center, 512/949–8068.

The seashore has joined with the Mexican government, other federal agencies, and the state of Texas in a research project to attempt to establish a nesting site on the beaches of Padre Island for the Kemp's Ridley Sea Turtle, the most endangered sea turtle. It is a multi-year endeavor. At this stage it is unlikely that you will see a turtle on the beach but if you do, notify seashore staff.

The Trails Take a walk along the three-quarter mile loop of the Grasslands Nature Trail and you will see dramatic evidence of the effect that constantly blowing strong winds has on the sands of Padre Island. The well-marked trail is located on the west side of the road about two miles from the park entrance. Most of it is accessible to the handicapped.

The trail winds through a "blowout" sand dune that has been stabilized by moisture and vegetation, and now provides sustenance for hardy island creatures. Not far from the trail there is a small, barren "blowout" dune actively migrating toward the lagoon. Trampling on the dune has prevented vegetation from gaining a foothold on the sands; therefore this dune is not resistant to the southeasterly winds.

Using an explanatory pamphlet available in a box at the trailhead as your guide, as you walk the trail keep a sharp eye out and you will be able to identify a variety of plants from Sea Oats to Whitestem Wildindigo and Partridge Pea, birds from Bobwhites to Killdeer, and animals such as Keeled Earless Lizard and Kangaroo rats.

Look for three or four live oak trees in the distance. They are the only trees remaining from what was once a large forest.

When you walk on the trail, take heed of the advice to wear shoes, use insect repellent, and stay on the path. The grasslands are home to the Western Diamondback Rattlesnake and the Western Massasauga Rattlesnake. They are dangerous and not easily seen.

Hunting, Fishing, And Boating The Intracoastal Waterway has been dredged to a depth of 14 feet to service commercial and pleasure boats. But most of the waters of Laguna Madre are shallow, averaging 4.5 feet. In the fall, great rafts of ducks and geese reach the end of the Central Flyway at this point and spend the winter at the lagoon's excellent feeding grounds. The seashore permits hunting during the migratory waterfowl season but *only* in the waters of the lagoon. For regulations that apply, write to the Superintendent of the seashore.

Fishing is popular at all times—deep sea fishing and fishing in the surf and in the lagoon. A Texas fishing license plus a salt water stamp is required for everyone except Texas residents sixteen and under or over sixty-five. Area convenience stores sell licenses. Sports fish common in the deep waters of the Gulf include kingfish, dolphin, bonita, red snapper, and sailfish. For information about boat charters, ask at the Malaquite Visitor Center.

Surf fishermen cast their lines into the surf from almost all parts of the beach seeking redfish, speckled sea trout, black drum, and whiting.

Boating is limited to the lagoon. Launching boats into the surf from Gulf beaches is prohibited. There is a boat launching ramp at Bird Island Basin and there are docks at both the Basin and Yarborough Pass. Redfish, black drum, and flounder are usually caught in the lagoon.

Boaters are cautioned not to go near South Bird Island. It is a bird sanctuary and nesting rookery for White Pelicans and a variety of colonial waterbirds. The seashore jointly works with the National Audubon Society to protect the sanctuary.

Oversand Vehicles (ORVs) Four-wheel drive vehicles may be driven on the beach anywhere except between the two roads that define the boundaries of Malaquite Beach. Because no services or telephones are available, drivers are urged to stock up on gas, water, and equipment to dig their vehicles out if they get stuck in the sand. Follow posted speed limits.

Only vehicles that are state licensed for street driving and are driven by licensed drivers are permitted. Before leaving, stop at the visitor center for pertinent information about driving conditions or call 512/949–8068.

Vehicles may not be driven between or on dunes, on grasslands, or on mudflats.

Pets Pets are not permitted at Malaquite Beach or posted areas. In other places, they must be on a leash and under physical control.

Historical/Cultural Resources Very little evidence remains of the culture of the past. Archeological research has revealed signs of Indian encampments and shipwrecks of Spanish explorers. Only the Novillo line camp complex, one of the stopping points on a cattle drive, recalls the island's ranching days. The complex, now deteriorating, can be seen in the distance on the Gulf side of the Park Road just before the road to Bird Island Basin. There are no historic sites to visit.

Mineral Exploration At Padre Island T h e
law authorizing Padre Island National Seashore specifically stated that the mineral rights then held by the state of Texas and by private owners could be reserved when the federal government acquired property. Consequently under the terms of this and other federal laws and regulations, such rights have been retained and leases have been granted for oil and gas production. Occasionally a seashore visitor will notice facilities associated with petroleum exploration and production. The seashore works closely with petroleum companies to ensure minimal disturbance of the environment as a result of drilling, production, or transportation.

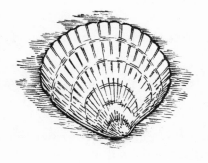

Padre Island National Seashore— A Special Adventure

Padre Island National Seashore is close to a big city and popular seaside resorts. Yet, among its vast, open spaces there are places where a person can know the uncertainty, the loneliness, the adventure of a frontier-like existence. The hardy, self-reliant beachgoer may find something here he has experienced nowhere else.

For Further Information, Contact:

Superintendent
Padre Island National Seashore
9405 South Padre Island Drive
Corpus Christi, TX 78418
Phone: 512/937–2621

Corpus Christi Convention and Tourist Bureau
Box 2664
Corpus Christi, TX 78403
 Phone: 512/882–5603 or 1/800/678–OCEAN
Texas residents: 1/800/221–SURF

Port Aransas Area Chamber of Commerce
Tourist and Convention Bureau
P.O. Box 356
Port Aransas, TX 78373
Phone: 1/800/221–9198 or
Texas residents: 1/800/242–3084

South Padre Island Visitor and Convention Bureau
P.O. Box 3500
South Padre Island, TX 78597
Phone: 1/800/343–2368
512/761–6433

Nueces County Padre Balli Park
10901 South Padre Island Drive
Cluster Box 3G
Corpus Christi, TX 78418
Phone: 512/949–8121

Mustang Island State Park
Box 326
Port Aransas, TX 78373
Phone: 512/749–5246

Cameron County Park System
Box 2106
South Padre Island, TX 78597
Phone: 512/761–5493

Point Reyes National Seashore

"We must take care to maintain the magic of Point Reyes . . . This wild shore . . . belongs wild. We share its wildness with the life that makes a permanent home here. We share its enchantment."

—**Stephen Trimble**
Point Reyes, The Enchanted Shore

"Jamai."[1] The Native American with the soft voice and gracious manner greeted us as we moved quietly about the Coast Miwok Indian village, trying not to disturb two deer nibbling on the grass at the compound's edge. This chance encounter (for it was not a weekend day when demonstrations of Indian life and crafts are given) lingers in our minds.

We listened to this gentle man describe the symbolism of the structural features of the earth-covered Indian meeting place; we learned about the life-fostering properties of

[1] Pomo Indian word of greeting both on arrival and departure, similar to the Hawaiian "Aloha."

acorns and bay and tule leaves; and we kept time to the beat of the Sati (a split stick rattle made from willow branches) as he danced and explained the significance of his movements. And we began to understand the culture of Point Reyes' first known human inhabitants.

Point Reyes has come full circle. Though sea adventurers, religious practitioners, and land entrepreneurs have had their day at Point Reyes, the enormous respect for all things natural that pervaded Coast Miwok Indian culture once again prevails on this magnificent "Island in Time."

Point Reyes—A Unique Seashore

Point Reyes is unique among national seashores. It is the only one on the West Coast. The prime attraction of all the others are barrier islands or spits formed by glacial remnants or sand deposits from the ocean. In contrast, Point Reyes National Seashore sits on a rocky land mass spotted with lakes, mountains, and marshes, which is, *for now,* a peninsula jutting out into the Pacific Ocean 30 miles north of San Francisco. It wasn't always there. Geographical evidence shows that many, many years ago—before recorded history—this odd-shaped chunk of the earth was much farther south—near Los Angeles.

Point Reyes is where it is today because of the violence of the earth's molten center. The peninsula is part of what geologists call the "Pacific plate," a segment of the earth's crust that has gradually been moving northward for 30 million years, bumping against the California coast, which is part of the "North American plate." When plates collide, startling things can happen. Scientists say that Point Reyes has been moving northward on the average of two to three inches a year relative to the rest of California. But there have been times when the "island" moved more rapidly. The most dramatic illustration in recent memory, of course, is in 1906 during the great San Francisco earthquake when tremendous pressures far below the earth's surface thrust it northward about 20 feet with catastrophic results along the San Andreas fault zone—the term used for the boundary area between the two plates.

One of the most fascinating experiences for the seashore visitor is to traverse the "Earthquake Trail"—right on the fault zone. Visual displays, including a fence moved 16 feet by the 1906 earthquake, help the layman to understand why Point Reyes is referred to as an "island in time."

Point Reyes National Seashore is not only different geologically from the seashore on the Atlantic and Gulf coasts; it varies in other ways. True, it has miles and miles of splendid beaches—but few can swim there. The water is cold and dangerous. Pacific "sneaker" waves (sudden, powerful, and dangerous waves) make it necessary to limit in-the-water activity at the "Great Beach." It has 145 miles of hiking trails suited to the beginner, the experienced hiker, or the rugged mountain climber. It offers an unusual opportunity to see wildlife in natural settings—native blacktailed deer, spotted axis and fallow deer,[2] tule elk, bobcats, mountain beaver; over 400 species of birds; seals, sea lions, and migrating whales. It has lakes and marshes, forested ridges, moors and grasslands. It has spectacular vistas —from mountain tops, coastal cliffs, and winding roads.

The northern point of Point Reyes, the peninsula, is separated from the California mainland by Tomales Bay which is directly over the San Andreas fault. On the western shore of Tomales Bay a state park and the town of Inverness lie between the Bay and the seashore's boundary.

[2] Spotted axis and fallow deer are non-native deer brought to Point Reyes by a local landowner in the 1940s. A surprising experience for a seashore visitor is the sight of a herd of white fallow deer leaping up a quiet hillside. White is one of the four color phases of these rare animals.

A few miles south of Inverness are the towns of Point Reyes Station and Olema, and beyond Olema, Golden Gate National Recreation Area, and the southeastern edge of the seashore. On the seashore's southern boundary is the community of Bolinas.

From the northern tip of Point Reyes a magnificent sweep of twenty miles of pristine beach arcs southwestward to the promontory from which the name Point Reyes is derived. From the promontory's headlands, the shore curves to the east, forming Drake's Bay, then south some 16 to 18 miles back to the California mainland.

Most of Point Reyes, over 70,000 acres, is within the national seashore. So long as present uses continue, lands used for communication facilities by the American Telephone and Telegraph Company, Radio Corporation of America, and the U.S. Coast Guard are exempt from park ownership. Several public utilities serving nearby communities and property owned by a religious organization, the Vedanta Society, are also exempt.

Part of Point Reyes National Seashore is rugged and densely vegetated, topped by mountainous Inverness Ridge. Most of this area is designated by Congress as a wilderness area. Lands classified as "wilderness" or "potential wilderness" occupy nearly half of the seashore's land. Here are luxuriant forests of Douglas firs over 200 feet high, bay trees, and great stands of rare Bishop pines.

Between the wilderness and the beaches are brushy hillsides and rolling grasslands on which beef and dairy cattle graze. Special permits allow the continuation of the agricultural practices that have been the major use of this land for 100 years.

Climate at the national seashore is a constant consideration in planning daily activities. Very frequently fog rolls in from the Pacific chilling the air west of Inverness Ridge, particularly in summer. The ridge acts as a barrier, though, and while people are hiking on trails or walking on the beach west of the ridge bundled up in sweaters and jackets, people on the east side may be basking in the sun. Winds blow strong on the headlands. They have been clocked at 133 miles an hour at Point Reyes lighthouse on the very tip; the average wind velocity is 40 miles an hour.

But these conditions should not discourage you. There are many clear, dry days, particularly in fall and spring when the vistas are great, the color of the wildflowers brilliant, and the air invigorating.

Point Reyes Before The National Seashore

The friendly Coast Miwok Indians who lived for hundreds of years in numerous small villages on Point Reyes welcomed their visitors from foreign lands and cultures. They gave them gifts and helped to sustain them while they repaired their ships.

Most renowned among the early foreign seafarers was Francis Drake, the English adventurer who is reported to have beached his ship , the *Golden Hinde,* on the shores of Drakes Bay in 1579 to get it in shape for crossing the Pacific in search of Far Eastern treasures. To this day, arguments are still being made to justify other nearby bays as the site of Captain Drake's haul-out. But the seashore appears to have accepted the evidence offered by the Point Reyes proponents. Point Reyes fits the description of the climate and land configurations in the journal kept by the ship's chaplain.

The whitish cliffs the English saw as they approached land reminded them of the cliffs of Dover back home and inspired Captain Drake to call the land "Nova Albion" (the first New England?). He is said to have interpreted the actions of the natives as evidence of their willingness to accept English rule and thereby claimed the land for Queen Elizabeth I. He never came back, however, and later explorers ignored his claim.

Spanish explorers left a more significant imprint than their English counterparts. A Spanish captain who had survived an earlier shipwrecked expedition sailed past the headlands after a rough, stormy day on January 6, 1603, the twelfth day of Christmas, the Feast of the Three Kings. He commemorated the occasion by naming it "La Punta de los Reyes." In time Americans modified the name to Point Reyes.

When Franciscan missionaries arrived in the area in the early nineteenth century, it was the beginning of the end for the traditional lifestyle of the Miwok Indians. They converted to the white man's religion, became part of a farming community, and contracted diseases for which they had no natural defenses. A few years later the government of Mexico, having achieved its independence from Spain, took over the missions and divided the land into very large, private parcels suitable for ranching. The Indians were not sufficiently prepared for the transition to a new way of life. Many perished and the culture of a people who for so many years had lived in harmony with land and sea disintegrated.

By treaty California became part of the United States in 1848. Not long after, three families from Vermont took over most of the land on Point Reyes. They leased it for dairy farming and beef cattle ranching which continues today on seashore land.

While farming flourished, a number of attempts were made to undertake other profitable ventures on the peninsula. Roads were built and a railroad route was established to attract travelers and commerce from the more populous east. An exclusive San Francisco club built a lodge on Bear Valley land, near Olema, and it became a popular base from which to hunt deer, bear, coyote, and mountain lion.

By the early 1940s, the land originally owned by the families of the enterprising New Englanders was in other hands, and plans had been made for development of deluxe private recreational retreats and facilities. But World War II put those plans on hold.

The Making Of The Point Reyes National Seashore

In anticipation of a future need for a significant national preserve of the diminishing, undeveloped seashore on the West Coast, the National Park Service eyed the vast expanse of wooded and pastoral land bordering the shores of Point Reyes and in 1935 recommended the purchase of 53,000 acres. No federal action was taken for a decade but the actions of conservation-minded residents of Marin County, in which Point Reyes is located, led to the establishment of county parks at Drakes Beach and McClures Beach, and on Tomales Bay.

After World War II, the start-up of logging activities on Inverness Ridge and the announcement of plans to sell vacation homesites overlooking Drakes Bay stirred renewed interest in a national seashore at Point Reyes. The proponents were opposed both by land developers and local ranchers who feared the loss of their livelihood. The writers of the proposed seashore legislation recognized the economic, esthetic, and educational value of the perpetuation of traditional ranching activity on Point Reyes, so they proposed the establishment of a 26,000 acre pastoral zone within the seashore. Landowners within the zone who were primarily engaged in agriculture could not be required to sell their land. Homeowners and ranchers who sold their land to the federal government could continue to live there for periods up to 50 years. They would be paid the fair market value of their property less an amount related to a specified term for their continued use of the land.

Pressure mounted and on September 13, 1962, a year after he had put his signature to the Cape Cod National Seashore authorizing legislation, President John F. Kennedy signed the law permitting the establishment of Point Reyes National Seashore "for purposes of public recreation, benefit and inspiration."

The Point Reyes National Seashore Today

The seashore today is living up to the challenge laid down by the far-sighted individuals who persisted in their cause. It took several years for the seashore to acquire the land—by donation, exchange, and purchase and time worked in favor of those who wanted Point Reyes to be a place of "inspiration." In 1972 the Golden Gate Recreation Area was established partially adjacent to Point Reyes and closer to San Francisco. This park serves as an outlet for active recreational pursuits, but in the northern portion next to Point Reyes the legislation encouraged the continuation of agriculture. The same advisory commission serves both parks.

Point Reyes lies within a heavily urbanized corridor of close to 5 million people and 79 percent to 80 percent of its over 2 million annual visitors come from the region. They come year-round to enjoy their own personal seashore delights—beach strolling, sunbathing, horseback riding, fishing, hiking, camping, taking pictures, and learning from the exhibits and seashore-sponsored programs.

How To Get There

Most people come to the seashore by car. From San Francisco, you can take the fastest route—north on California Highway 101, then west on Sir Francis Drake Boulevard through Samuel P. Taylor State Park to Olema, where signs point to the Bear Valley Visitor Center one-half mile west.

If you have time and have never driven it, take the scenic route. Leave Highway 101 4.5 miles north of the Golden Gate Bridge and take California Highway 1 to

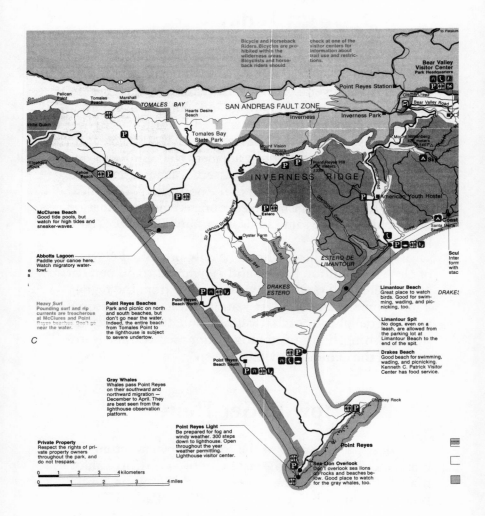

Bicycle and Horseback Riders. Bicycles are prohibited within the wilderness areas. Bicyclists and horseback riders should check at one of the visitor centers for information about trail use and restrictions.

Bear Valley Visitor Center
Park Headquarters

Point Reyes Station

Bear Valley Road

TOMALES BAY

SAN ANDREAS FAULT ZONE

Inverness   Inverness Park

Pelican Point   Tomales   Marshall
Beach   Beach

Hearts Desire Beach

White Gulch

Tomales Bay State Park

Mount Vision

INVERNESS RIDGE

Point Reyes Hill

American Youth Hostel

Pierce Point Road

Elephant Rock

Kehoe Beach

Estero

Coast

McClures Beach
Good tide pools, but watch for high tides and sneaker-waves.

Sir Francis Drake Highway

Oyster Farm

ESTERO DE LIMANTOUR

Abbotts Lagoon
Paddle your canoe here. Watch migratory waterfowl.

DRAKES ESTERO

Limantour Beach
Great place to watch birds. Good for swimming, wading, and picnicking, too.

DRAKE

Heavy Surf
Pounding surf and rip currents are treacherous at McClures and Point Reyes beaches. Don't go near the water.

C

Point Reyes Beaches
Park and picnic on north and south beaches, but don't go near the water. Indeed, the entire beach from Tomales Point to the lighthouse is subject to severe undertow.

Point Reyes Beach North

Limantour Spit
No dogs, even on a leash, are allowed from the parking lot at Limantour Beach to the end of the spit.

Drakes Beach
Good beach for swimming, wading, and picnicking. Kenneth C. Patrick Visitor Center has food service.

Point Reyes Beach South

Gray Whales
Whales pass Point Reyes on their southward and northward migration — December to April. They are best seen from the lighthouse observation platform.

Chimney Rock

Point Reyes Light
Be prepared for fog and windy weather. 300 steps down to lighthouse. Open throughout the year weather permitting. Lighthouse visitor center.

Point Reyes

Private Property
Respect the rights of private property owners throughout the park, and do not trespass.

Sea Lion Overlook
Don't overlook sea lions on rocks and beaches below. Good place to watch for the gray whales, too.

0   1   2   3   4 kilometers
0   1   2   3   4 miles

check at one of the visitor centers for information about trail use and restrictions.

Bear Valley Visitor Center
Park Headquarters

Point Reyes Station

Olema

Samuel P. Taylor State Park

to San Francisco and San Rafael

to Petaluma

North

Golden Gate National Recreation Area
(Olema Valley area managed by Point Reyes NS)

SAN ANDREAS FAULT ZONE

Olema Creek

Bear Valley Road

Inverness Park

Five Brooks

Mount Wittenberg
1407

Bear

Coast

Coast Creek

Sky

Palomarin

RIDGE

Point Reyes Hill
1336

American Youth Hostel

Coast

Santa Maria Beach

Point Resistance

Kelham Beach

Wildcat

Wildcat Beach

Wildcat Camp

Crystal Lake

Bass Lake

Pelican Lake

Alamere Falls

Double Point
Stormy Stack

Abalone Point

ESTERO DE LIMANTOUR

DRAKES BAY

Limantour Beach
Great place to watch birds. Good for swimming, wading, and picnicking, too.

Sculptured Beach
Interesting geological formations—folded shale with caves, tunnels, and stacks.

Arch Rock
Bear Valley trail ends here. Crawl through the sea tunnel at low tide.

Steep Cliffs
Cliffs of Point Reyes are likely to crumble and slide. Climbing on them or walking near the edge invites catastrophe and a possible fine.

Point Reyes Bird Observatory
Independent research facility.

Waters adjacent to the seashore boundaries are within the Point Reyes/Farallon Islands National Marine Sanctuary. Information on the sanctuary is available at the seashore visitor centers.

Limantour Spit
No dogs, even on a leash, are allowed from the parking lot at Limantour Beach to the end of the spit.

Drakes Beach
Good beach for swimming, wading, and picnicking. Kenneth C. Patrick Visitor Center has food service.

OCEAN

Chimney Rock

Point Reyes

Sea Lion Overlook
Don't overlook sea lions on rocks and beaches below. Good place to watch for the gray whales, too.

National Park Service Boundary

Boundary for Private Property

Wilderness Area, Potential Wilderness Area, and Research Natural Area

Restrooms

Telephone

Ranger Station

Parking

Picnic Area

Backcountry camping

Fishing

Interpretive Trail

Stables

Dogs and pets on leash

Olema. If you do and you've never seen California red-
woods, you will be tempted to detour at the sign for Muir
Woods National Monument and enjoy a walk through
these awesome giants of the California coast. If you take
this route between March and mid-July on a weekend or
holiday, you may also want to stop at Audubon Canyon
Ranch 3 miles north of Stinson Beach. This thousand acre
ranch is a major breeding place for Great Blue Herons and
Great Egrets. The public is welcome at certain times. For
details, write to Audubon Canyon Ranch.

Where To Stay

Private Accommodations There are a few
motels in the towns close to the seashore as well as several
bed and breakfast inns. It is important to make reservations. For information about what is available write The
Inns of Point Reyes. If nothing is available, check major
motel chains for accommodations in towns along Highway
101.
   Meals are not a problem. There are a number of restaurants in Inverness, Olema, and Point Reyes Station. If
you wish to spend a leisurely day at Point Reyes National
Seashore, take your lunch with you. The nearby towns
have convenience stores where you can pick up take-out
food. The only food concession within the seashore is at
Drakes Beach. It is open daily from 10 a.m. to 6 p.m.

Camping There are four hike-in campgrounds at
the seashore—all approached from the Bear Valley Trailhead. Sky Camp is on the western side of Mt. Wittenberg,
a 2.25 mile hike from the trailhead. Coast Camp is on a
grassy bluff above the beach, almost 9 miles from the trailhead. A 5 mile hike will take you to Glen Camp in a small
wooded valley. Wildcat Camp is on a grassy meadow near

a stream, about 6 miles from the trailhead. Wood fires are prohibited. Only charcoal, gas stoves, or canned heat may be used. There are pit toilets, picnic tables, and poles on which to hang food to keep it away from raccoons and foxes.

These are the only places within the seashore where camping of any kind is allowed. Permits are required. They can be obtained at the Bear Valley Visitor Center. There is no charge. Wildcat is reserved for group camping—maximum two nights. Camping at other campgrounds is limited to one night each.

If you want to camp and hike-in camping is not for you, the Samuel P. Taylor State Park at Lagunitas, a few miles from Olema, maintains sixty-three campsites. Hot showers, flush toilets, and water are available. Reservations are required. For information, contact the Samuel P. Taylor State Park. Staff at the Bear Valley Visitor Center can provide information about private campgrounds and about the seashore's youth hostel facility.

What To Do At Point Reyes

The Visitor Center There is so much to do at Point Reyes, try to allow for more than a day's visit. A first-time visitor should start by going to the impressive Bear Valley Visitor Center, a half mile from Olema. This handsome rugged structure set in a beautiful valley surrounded by rolling hills sets the mood for a step back in time. Here is a perfect way station where pressures of twentieth century living fade away and a fascinating story of natural creatures and events absorbs the mind and spirit.

The building, like many other things you will enjoy at Point Reyes, is the embodiment of the vision of thousands of West Coast citizens who saw Point Reyes as a rare resource that should be available to all citizens. It was built in 1983 at a cost of 1.5 million dollars—all donated funds.

See the audio-visual program about Point Reyes. Look at the exhibits depicting native flora, fauna, and sea life. Study the seismograph monitoring earthquake activity throughout the world. Browse through the bookstore. Talk with the rangers about the weather and the trails and get a monthly schedule of events—ranger-led walks, canoe trips, and tours.

You may want to come back to the visitor center after you've been to the other attractions nearby—the Earthquake Trail, Kule Loklo, the Coast Miwok Indian cultural exhibit, the Morgan Horse Ranch, or the Bear Valley hiking trail. It's delightful to sit by the fireplace in comfortable chairs and look out the big windows at a covey of California quail pecking at the ground or deer grazing on the hillside. The center is open 9 a.m. to 5 p.m. Monday through Friday, 8 a.m. to 5 p.m. on weekends.

The Earthquake Trail along the San Andreas fault zone is just a short walk from the visitor center. It is a self-guiding trail, a little over one-half mile long, that is completely accessible to wheelchairs—thanks to the many volunteers who donated money and labor. Signs along the way explain what happened in 1906 to the land on which you walk.

Back to the parking lot. Walk uphill along the Woodpecker trail to the Morgan Horse Ranch. This special breed of small, friendly, calm-natured, and strong horses, is considered the only true American horse. All are descended from a horse owned by Justin Morgan in 1795. An exhibit in a small red barn tells the story of the horse from colonial days to now. Morgan horses are raised and trained here for use by rangers throughout the National Park System. Volunteers spend many hours working with them and putting on demonstrations for visitors.

Near the visitor center you will see signs directing you to Kule Loklo, the Coast Miwok Indian words for Bear Valley. A half mile walk up a wooded trail will take you to this interpretive model of an early Miwok village. Much of it was built by volunteers. If you are there on a weekend, you will probably see rangers and volunteers demonstrating arrow-making and basket weaving.

What you do next depends on whether you want to visit the beaches or the lighthouse, hike, bike-ride, ride a horse, or just drive and drink in the scenery.

The Beaches You have a choice. To get to the "Great Beach" facing the Pacific Ocean or Drakes Beach on the Bay, take Sir Francis Drake Highway from Olema. The highway goes north through Inverness, then curves west. There are turnoffs to Point Reyes Beach North and Point Reyes Beach South where you can park, picnic, use restrooms, and walk the beach for miles. Because of the severe undertow, do not go too near the water. "Sneaker" waves, at times least expected, court disaster.

If you want to swim, take the turn-off to the left, between North and South Beaches, to Drakes Beach. Even here the water is pretty cold. There are no lifeguards at any of the beaches. Fishing is permitted (California license required.) There is a visitor center with exhibits and restrooms, and a cafe.

Swimming at your own risk is also permitted at Limantour Beach which can be reached by taking the Limantour Road from Bear Valley Road near the visitor center.

Other beaches may be reached by hiking some of the scenic trails, some long and strenuous, some suitable for the novice.

The water is much warmer in Tomales Bay which is relatively free from wind and fog. Local residents, therefore, prefer to swim at the beaches in Tomales Bay State Park, just north of Inverness. For information, write Tomales Bay State Park.

SCUBA Diving SCUBA diving in the waters around the head of Tomales Bay is discouraged because of the presence of Great White Sharks which have been known to attack swimmers and divers in this area.

Point Reyes Lighthouse The most popular destination of all visitors to Point Reyes is the lighthouse area—especially in clear weather and when there is a chance of seeing the grey whales migrating from Alaska to Baja California in late December, January, and February and back again in March and April. Although they can be seen from other points along the Great Beach, this is the place where the view is the best. On any sunny weekend in January and February, traffic can be backed up for miles.

But the trip to the lighthouse is well worth it at other times also. A short walk from the lighthouse parking area takes you to a point overlooking sea lions frolicking and barking in the water and on the rocks below. Another short walk will take you to the very tip of the point where, if the weather is clear, you can enjoy a magnificent view. You may see the Farallon Islands, twenty miles out to sea. The waters between Point Reyes and the Farallons are part of a national marine sanctuary and the water is protected for marine related life.

From this point, you will also see pelicans, common murres, and other seabirds, flying about or resting on the rocks. Don't go too near the edge of the cliff; the rocks are not stable and you can easily fall.

If it is open and weather permits, you can walk the 300 steps down to the lighthouse. The lighthouse was built in 1870 halfway down the cliff because, if built at the top, the fog at times would make it impossible for its beam to be visible at sea. This point is the foggiest and certainly one of the windiest places on the West Coast. Although the light and foghorn are now automated, the original light mechanism, with its rare Fresnel lens, is still operable.

The lighthouse and lighthouse visitor center are open to the public Thursday through Monday, 10 a.m. to 5 p.m., weather permitting. Restrooms are available. At several points along the stairway to the lighthouse, there are platforms where visitors can rest.

It's a 21 mile drive to the lighthouse from Bear Valley Visitor Center. Before leaving, you may want to call the lighthouse visitor center to see if it is open. (Phone: 415/669-1534.)

On your return from the lighthouse, take a detour at the sign for Chimney Rock and visit the point where Drakes Bay and the Pacific meet. Here is where the old life saving station served as a base for many attempted rescues of ships and men in trouble. Sailing along the California coast has always been extremely hazardous in bad weather. There are fifty-six known shipwrecks. The station is in the process of being restored and is not open to the public, but you can enjoy a sweeping view of the area where the cliffs and beach meet the bay.

Trails—For Hikers, Bikers, And Horseback Riders

There is a trail for every level of hiking ability and in all parts of the park—in the mountains and meadows, along beaches on Drakes Bay, along Drakes and Limantour Esteros, to five quiet lakes in the wilderness area, to Mc-Clures and Kehoe Beaches and Abbott's Lagoon on the Pacific and through the moors and meadows of the Tule Elk Range to Tomales Point. For details, pick up a trail map at Bear Valley Visitor Center. For the dedicated hiker, there are two excellent books by avid hikers: *Point Reyes* by Dorothy L. Whitnah and *Exploring Point Reyes* by Phil Arnot and Elvira Monroe. They are on sale at the visitor center bookstore. Both books contain personal appraisals of the sights, experiences, and joys of numerous trails.

Bicycle riding the trails of Point Reyes has been a popular activity for many years. A recent Park Service ruling has led to the prohibition of bicycles in wilderness areas. This has stirred up considerable controversy. For current information, check with the rangers who will also be able to tell you where bicycles can be rented.

There is a specially designated horse trail starting near the Bear Valley Visitor Center. Check with the rangers for other trails on which horses are permitted and current information on stables where you can rent horses.

Driving Through The Park A drive on any road through the park is an enjoyable experience and offers an opportunity to see uncommon wildlife. Here are some drives not previously mentioned you may want to take.

A few miles after Sir Francis Drake Highway turns west, turn left at a sign marked for Mt. Vision. This winding, hilly road skirts Inverness Ridge. You will travel partly through dense woods, partly in the open with views of Point Reyes' many rolling hills. Fallow deer, some white, some brown, blacktailed, and axis deer graze in this area. Bobcats may cross your path. Many species of Point Reyes' unusual complement of birdlife can be seen. In spring, wild flowers—lupines, Indian paintbrush, iris—all shapes and colors abound. In clear weather there are magnificent views of the esteros and beaches from the crest.

Farther along on Drakes Highway, opposite the tall antennas of overseas radio receiving stations, turn left for a short drive to Johnson's Oyster Farm. This is a family business, here before the national seashore, operating under a long term lease to continue an unusual form of oyster culture Johnson learned in Japan. You can watch the operation, pick up a free explanatory pamphlet and, if you are prepared, buy oysters to cook on the beach.

Don't miss the Pierce Point Road leading to the Tule Elk Range which occupies 2600 acres at the northern tip of Point Reyes. When traveling the Drake Highway out of Inverness instead of turning west toward the lighthouse, follow the signs for Pierce Point Road. You will see deer in the open meadows and, finally, you may be rewarded by the sight of a herd of tule elk, a native species reintroduced to the seashore under protected conditions in 1978. During the rutting season in the fall, listen for the haunting bugle of a bull elk laying down a challenge to his rivals.

To get to the southern end of the seashore, take California Highway 1 south. Then take the Olema-Bolinas Road and just short of Bolinas, turn right at the sign for the Point Reyes Bird Observatory (PRBO). PRBO is a non-profit, ornithological research and educational organization located just within the boundaries of the seashore. It focuses on birds and marine mammals of the Pacific. Its Palomarin Field Station, located here, is open to the public at certain times. For more information, write to the observatory. Shortly after you pass the PRBO, the road stops at the seashore's Palomarin Trailhead.

Educational Programs The short-term visitor can learn much about the past and present of Point Reyes from the exhibits, books, and pamphlets at the visitor centers and from talking with the rangers. But for those who want to partake of them, there are other opportunities to expand their knowledge and gain firsthand experience with the seashore's unusual environment.

The monthly schedule of naturalist activities lists ranger led walks, boat rides, and other activities of a few hours' duration. Other seashore sponsored educational experiences include week-long programs for school children, four to five week-long summer camp programs, elderhostel programs, and weekend field seminars that draw upon the expertise of persons associated with the many research and educational institutions in the San Francisco area. Many environmental organizations sponsor hikes and programs at the seashore. For information, write the Superintendent, Point Reyes National Seashore.

Most of the educational programs are held at the Point Reyes/Clem Miller Environmental Education Center located off Limantour Road in a new privately funded

$600,000.00 facility which replaced a World War II quonset hut previously used for this purpose.

Fishing And Hunting
Fishing is permitted on the lakes, marshes, and beaches of Point Reyes. Persons sixteen or over are required to have a California fishing license. Bass and Sacramento perch are most common. The seashore is attempting to reintroduce salmon and steelhead which were native to Point Reyes but disappeared some time ago.

No hunting is permitted.

Oversand Vehicles (ORVs)
No off-road driving is permitted anywhere within the seashore.

Pets
Because of their potential threat to wildlife at the seashore, dogs are not permitted on trails or in campgrounds. You may take pets on leashes to certain *designated* beaches and other places in the park. Check with the rangers for current regulations.

Historical/Cultural Resources
Several Point Reyes sites and structures have been judged to be of such historical significance that the necessary steps have been taken to place them on the National Register of Historic Places. The Point Reyes Lifeboat Station and The Olema Lime Kilns are presently listed on the register and the lighthouse and Pierce Point Ranch have been nominated. Others under consideration are the Home Ranch and five archeological districts: Tomales Point, Headlands, Double Point Coast, Drakes Estero and Bear Valley. An official Historic Resources study has been done.

Point Reyes National Seashore—Restoring A Natural Wonderland

When the seashore staff set out several years ago to preserve and, in some cases, restore the native bounty of Point Reyes, they laid many plans to research, monitor, and take positive steps to reintroduce native species. There has been progress. The tule elk are now thriving. Efforts to prevent exotic (non-native) animals (fallow and axis deer) and plants (Scotch broom, water hyacinths, eucalyptus, and pampas grass among others) from interfering with the health of native species are ongoing. There is evidence that the reintroduction of salmon and steelhead is having some success. Measures to control erosion on ranch land are under way. The land, marshes, forests, and shores continue to be hospitable sites for land and shore birds alike—over 400 species recorded to date.

In cooperation with the National Marine Fisheries Service and the California Department of Fish and Game, the national seashore works to protect the marine mammals who live or spend time in the water adjacent to Point Reyes and on its beaches. California and northern sea lions, harbor seals, and northern elephant seals, the southern sea otter, and the California Gray Whale are the objects of much study and attention.

Part of California's natural wonderland is its magnificent coastline and its residents, appreciating this, are determined to keep as much of it as possible from being despoiled. Fortunately for the residents of the other 49 states, there is within that state a grand and glorious patch of land and seacoast known as Point Reyes National Seashore that belongs to all of us. Go there and enjoy the west coast's only national seashore.

For Further Information, Contact:

Superintendent
Point Reyes National Seashore
Point Reyes, CA 94956
Phone: 415/663–8522

The Inns of Point Reyes
Box 145
Inverness, CA 94937
Phone: 415/663–1420

Tomales Bay State Park
Star Route
Inverness CA 94937
Phone: 415/669–1140

Samuel P. Taylor State Park
P.O. Box 251
Lagunitas, CA 94938
Phone: 415/488–9897
Campsite reservations: 1/800/444–7275

Audubon Canyon Ranch
4990 Shoreline Highway
Stinson Beach, CA 94970
Phone: 415/868–9244

Point Reyes Bird Observatory
4900 Shoreline Highway
Stinson Beach, CA 94970
Phone: 415/868–0655

The Anatomy Of The Beach

Sand, Wind and Wave

The ocean beach evokes some of man's deepest, primitive, perhaps primordial, emotions. To stand on the beach and watch the restless sands as they remold footsteps into featureless dimples, to drink in the rushing, stimulating air laden with the tantalizing aromas of the shore, to sense the power of the sea in its surging, pounding breakers as they march in ranks to their doom in the sand, to see the last dark ribbon of wave on the far horizon that seems to be on the edge of an abyss, is to experience an exhilaration of spirit that overwhelms the senses. Worldly care and tribulation sink below the level of consciousness. We lose ourselves as we sense the fateful, relentless conflict between sand, wind, and wave.

Sometimes there is calm—the sea, blue and rippling; the wind, mere zephyr; the sand, bright and warm. At other times there is furious combat.

Anyone who has witnessed a roaring nor'easter, much less a full hurricane, can attest to the utter violence and stupefying power of a wind and sea seemingly gone mad. Yet it is, perhaps, knowledge of that violent side of the beach, its wrath, its consummate power to destroy man's works, that heightens its allure.

The Rising Oceans

Sand, wind, and wave—some of the effects of their dynamic movement are readily seen and measured in hours, in days, or in years. Sand dunes can change height and shape between weekend visits. We sail casually today across open waters where a sandy spit or island stood but a few years ago. Ponderous masonry seawalls are reduced to rubble by a single winter storm. Such effects of storm-driven sand, wind, and wave are direct and easy to comprehend.

Short term change in the surface of the ocean is also familiar to us. The waves we watch crashing on the beach are the result of wind molding hills and furrows in the water. The rising and falling of the ocean level each day results from tides caused by the varying gravitational effects of the positions of the moon and the sun in relation to the earth. Occasionally these tides rise to extreme levels due to an effect called storm surge caused by the low atmospheric pressure accompanying coastal storms. Such short term changes in ocean water levels persist for hours or, at most, a few days.

There is a longer term change in the level of the ocean that is not so easily detected or quantified. This is the rising of the worldwide ocean levels—in effect a deepening of the oceans that, if continued, will engulf our present coastlines.

The level of the world's oceans has been rising and falling slowly for tens of thousands of years. Long ago the level of the oceans was much higher than at present. Then ocean levels fell far below that of today. Now the oceans are rising again. Oceanographers have ample evidence that the ocean level today is hundreds of feet higher than it was thousands of years ago. Although they agree that ocean levels are now still rising, they are not certain of the current rate of rising or of the causes.

Dr. Stephen P. Leatherman in his *Barrier Island Handbook* says this about eustatic (worldwide) sea level rise:

> *While melting of the polar ice caps continues to be a major cause of rising sea level, the rate of rise is expected to accelerate in the future due to increasing global temperatures, driven by higher levels of carbon dioxide in the atmosphere. Due to the "greenhouse effect," higher average global temperatures could result in as much as a six foot rise within the next 100 years, which would be catastrophic for major cities located in low-lying coastal areas (e.g. Washington, D.C., London).*

It is this advance of the level of the oceans continuing around the clock, around the years, around the centuries, that is truly the wave of the future for our beaches, coasts, and coastal plains.

Barriers and Beaches

Much of the United States mainland, from the mighty ledges of Maine to the bayou country of Louisiana, is exposed directly to the power of the sea. Its headlands, beaches, and ledges have little recourse but to stand fast in the face of storms and rising sea levels and suffer the gradual drowning of their forward ranks.

Twenty-seven hundred miles of the shoreline, however, from Canada to the Mexican border, is protected from the direct ocean-front conditions by an almost unbroken line of off shore islands, spits, and peninsulas generally referred to as coastal barriers. These barriers have one thing in common—a beach which is their frontier with the open sea.

The origin of coastal barriers lies deep in our geological past. Current theory identifies several events that were involved: melting of the prehistoric glaciers that deposited vast quantities of sand and gravel off the shores of New England and New York; rising ocean levels that turned shore front ridges into islands off the mid-Atlantic coast; and the pushing of underwater shoals of sand into ridges above water level by ocean currents in the Gulf of Mexico.

A coastal barrier is a dynamic system. Constantly reacting to the onslaught of the sea, it grows larger or smaller, wider or narrower, longer or shorter. Sometimes it fragments into islands which, over time, rejoin into a peninsula. Moreover, the barrier saves itself from inundation as the sea level rises *by retreating toward the mainland!* See Figure 1 reprinted from *Barrier Island Handbook*, courtesy of Stephen P. Leatherman.

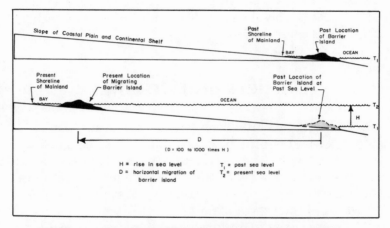

In the words of Dr. Orrin H. Pilkey Jr. in his book *The Beaches Are Moving:*

> As sea level continued to rise, it drove the islands up the continental shelf. How fast a given island moves is controlled by how fast sea level rises and by the slope of the coastal plain over which the island moves. Along the Gulf Coast the coastal plain was so flat the islands must have moved one hundred feet a year at

*times. Naturally, the mainland shoreline behind the
islands retreated too.*

Bordering the Atlantic and Gulf coastlines to a distance up to a hundred miles out to sea lies the continental
shelf, a part of the continent that once was dry land but is
now covered by the oceans' rising waters. Beyond the shelf
the ocean bottom drops quickly to great depths. The shelf
itself is relatively shallow, sloping upward toward the coast
at an average rate of one foot in 540 feet, as determined by
oceanographer Willard Bascom. This gradual upward slope
is the basic mechanism that keeps the beach as well as the
rest of the barrier island from being drowned by the inexorable rise in the level of the sea.

In moving toward the mainland the barrier island, in
effect, rolls over itself. Where oceanfront beach lies today
a maritime forest grew years ago. Figure 2, reprinted from
Barrier Island Handbook, courtesy of Stephen P. Leatherman, shows the stumps of trees studding one such beach.
This barrier migration results from a combination of inlet
breaching (where the sea cuts a channel through the barrier), aeolian sand (windblown sand), and storm overwash
(waves overtopping the dunes).

Scientists who specialize in the study and interpretation of the earth's dryland and ocean bottom surface features (they are called geomorphologists), consider inlet

formation to be a driving force for barrier movement. Only occasionally is overwash so powerful and prolonged that it creates an inlet, sometimes a navigable one, through a barrier system. Usually overwash lasts only as long as the storm tidal surge lasts and ceases with the return to normal tidal conditions. Overwashes all rearrange the island to some degree and seem to be a contributor to the mechanism that moves the barrier system toward the mainland.

Geomorphologists can look at the present configuration of a barrier system and tell us where inlets have occurred in the past. And they can predict, by extension, where overwash is likely to occur in the future. Residents of densely developed barrier beaches are acutely aware that certain areas of those beaches have been identified as highly susceptible to future storm overwash and possible new inlet formation.

Although the beach is only one feature of a barrier island system, it is the one element that attracts the most attention. It is also the critical element of the barrier complex, which typically includes an estuary, lagoon, salt or fresh water marsh, maritime forest, and back dunes in any combination. These barrier elements are there because the beach is there to protect them by acting as a buffer to the high energy ocean surf.

The barrier island complex forms a natural environment of critical importance. This complex system provides physical protection to much of the heavily populated coastline. Equally important, it provides and protects a vast ecological habitat for the lower reaches of the food chain on which our national bounty of sea food, wildfowl, small mammals, and songbirds utterly depends. If we were to lose the barrier island features usually referred to as wetlands, the economic and social impact would be catastrophic. And it is the health of the beach itself on which this bountiful habitat depends for its life.

Barriers and Man

Attempts to control or to exploit coastal barriers, spurred by housing and resort interests, have been going on for a long time. These attempts have increased over the past several years. However, as evidence of the hazards of developing barrier systems has mounted, so has the controversy over the social and political policy regarding their management.

Housing and resort developers draw on vast private and public resources, money, and material to build structures on some coastal barriers, despite all the evidence that the construction of roads, buildings, and other structures interferes with the natural coastward migration of the barrier. This, in turn, threatens the continuance of the barrier system and the social and economic health of our coasts. Moreover, such construction itself is subject to the hazards of rising sea levels and powerful storms.

Scientists point out that most of the heavy development on the east coast barrier beaches has taken place in the last twenty-five years. It has also been a period in which the frequency and severity of hurricanes have been far below average. They fear that when the odds begin to even out, a disaster will occur on the Atlantic coast similar to the destruction unleashed on Galveston, Texas in 1900, when a hurricane killed thousands of people and destroyed most of the city.

Hurricane Gloria, as it moved toward the mid-Atlantic coast in September of 1985, was of great concern to meteorologists. The destructive potential of the intense winds and the extremely low barometric pressure of the eye of this storm seemed to spell appalling disaster for shore areas from the Carolinas to New England. Disaster there was but, luckily, nothing approaching the level that might well have resulted if the path of the storm had been different by a few miles.

Scientists also have raised serious questions about the use of bulkheads, groins, and similar steel, masonry, and concrete installations to protect developed barrier beaches. Recent experience indicates the futility of such attempts to offset the inexorable rising of the sea level. For the seas, as they have for thousands of years, continue to rise and push farther up the continental shelf. The barrier beaches, as they have for thousands of years, move toward the mainland, maintaining their elevation above the encroaching sea by also moving, retreating, and pushing up the continental shelf.

Scientists are not the only people concerned about the future of the coastal barriers. Local officials in the heavily developed communities astride the barriers face increasing problems of diminishing beaches and damaged structures. Congress views costs associated with coastal barrier development—such as potential liability under the federal flood insurance program— as a possible enormous drain on the national budget.

Though they share common geological features, the coastal barriers cannot be treated alike. Social and political circumstances call for alternate approaches to their future management.

Some barriers have already been substantially developed. They range from such intensely developed cities as Miami Beach, Florida, Ocean City, Maryland, and Atlantic City, New Jersey to more moderately developed islands such as Dauphin Island, Alabama and Hilton Head, South Carolina. The critical question for these places is how to survive in something like their present form despite the unyielding march of natural processes. Engineering ingenuity may delay these processes but ultimately it can not stop them. The future may reduce the options. Such developed communities on barrier islands may have to do what earlier residents of now deserted islands did: relocate to the mainland.

There are coastal barriers under private ownership that are undeveloped. What might become of them? Will some become like Miami Beach or Ocean City? Will others become federal parks? The United States Congress, recognizing the urgency of the coastal barrier problem, enacted the Coastal Barrier Resources Act (CBRA) in 1982. This act established the Coastal Barrier Resources System (CBRS) and identified a proposed network of 186 undeveloped barrier units along the Atlantic and Gulf coasts of the United States. The intent of this legislation is to prohibit the use of federal funds to aid future development of these barriers. Federal National Flood Insurance and federal funds for construction of roads, bridges, utility systems, and jetties, would all be denied where they would assist development on the privately owned, undeveloped barriers in the CBRS. A new Miami Beach or Ocean City might be developed on these barriers, but only without any expenditure of federal funds. It is likely, also, that no federal funds would be available to sustain future development on the CBRS barrier units, such as the funds for beach nourishment expended at Miami Beach and proposed for Ocean City.

There is another category of barrier beach system—those that are now under public control. Barriers controlled by state or local governments, mostly as recreation areas, are generally being administered wisely and protected from development. The federally controlled barriers, most of which are the focus of this book, are administered by various agencies of the federal government, primarily by the National Park Service.

Barriers as National Seashores

Comprising one-fifth of the coastal barriers of the Atlantic and Gulf coasts, the national seashores have come under national stewardship through a variety of circumstances over the past half century. Evolving National Park Service policy, dedicated civilian experts and seashore staff, and the increased knowledge and interest of the public have combined to make the seashores a textbook case of how best to manage a precious natural coastal resource.

In the early seventies the National Park Service, as the result of research, expert advice, and observation of the results of their own seashore management practices, decided that the piecemeal attempts of the past to "stabilize the beaches" were not only ineffectual but were also counterproductive in maintaining the health of the beach and its wetlands, bays, and estuaries.

The current policy is to avoid any structures, development, and facilities other than those limited in number and extent to the minimum needed for public recreation. Simply stated, the National Park Service is convinced that a flexible policy is the best way to protect the natural environment, minimize danger to life and property, and manage the national seashores effectively and economically. Wherever practicable, the policy is to let nature take its course, avoid confrontation with the sea, and accept the free migration of the beaches that keeps the seashores healthy.

CHECKLIST

ACTIVITIES	Cape Cod	Fire Island	Assateague Island	Cape Hatteras	Cape Lookout	Cumberland Island	Canaveral	Gulf Islands	Padre Island	Point Reyes
Camping:	1									
Primitive		X	X		X	X	X	X	X	X
Family	X	X	X	X		X		X	X	
Motor Home	X		2	2				X	2	
Hiking:										
Beachcombing	X	X	X	X	X	X	X	X	X	X
Remote Area		X			X	X	X	X	X	X
Easy Track	X	X	X	X	X	X	X	X	X	X
Swimming:										
Family	X	X	X	X	3	3	3	X	X	3
SCUBA/Snorkeling		X		X	X			4		
Surfing		X	X	X	X		X	4	X	
Exploration:										
Audio/Visual	X	X	X	X		X	X	X		X
Ranger Program	X	X	X	X	X	X	X	X	X	X
Nature Trail	X	X	X	X	X	X	X	X	X	X
Historic Site	X	X	5	X	X	X	X	X	5	X
Hunting	X	X	X	X	X	6	X	4	X	
Fishing	X	X	X	X	X	X	X	X	X	X
Off-Road Driving	7	7	7	7	7				7	
Bicycling	X		X				X	X	X	X
Horseback Riding	X		8				X	4	X	X

1—Private grounds only within seashore boundaries
2—No utility connections
3—No lifeguards
4—Florida district only
5—Not open to public
6—Managed hunts only
7—Restrictions apply
8—Permitted except from May 10th to October 15th (insect season)
9—Mississippi district only

CHECKLIST

	Cape Cod	Fire Island	Assateague Island	Cape Hatteras	Cape Lookout	Cumberland Island	Canaveral	Gulf Islands	Padre Island	Point Reyes
ACCESSIBILITY										
Direct Road Access	X	X	X	X			X	X	X	X
Ferry Access:										
Pedestrian		X		X	X	X		9		
Vehicles				X	X					
Boat		X	X	X	X	X	X	X	X	
NEARBY FACILITIES										
Family Camping	X	X	X	X	X	X	X	X	X	X
Motor Home Park	X	X			X	X	X	X	X	
Motels/Hotels	X	X	X	X	X	X	X	X	X	X
SEASONALITY										
High-Use Months:										
January										
February										
March							X			
April						X	X	X		
May						X	X	X	X	X
June	X		X	X	X	X	X	X	X	X
July	X	X	X	X	X	X	X	X	X	X
August	X	X	X	X	X	X	X	X		X
September	X		X	X	X	X	X	X		
October				X	X	X				
November										
December										

1—Private grounds only within seashore boundaries
2—No utility connections
3—No lifeguards
4—Florida district only
5—Not open to public
6—Managed hunts only
7—Restrictions apply
8—Permitted except from May 10th to October 15th (insect season)
9—Mississippi district only

Directory Of Information

About Visiting Cape Cod National Seashore

Details About Programs And Facilities

Superintendent
Cape Cod National Seashore
South Wellfleet, MA 02663
Phone: 508/340–3785

Overnight Accommodations

Cape Cod Chamber of Commerce
Junction Routes 6 and 132
Hyannis, MA 02601
Phone: 508/362–3225

Camping

Superintendent
Cape Cod National Seashore
South Wellfleet, MA 02663
Phone: 508/340–3785

Park Supervisor
Roland E. Nickerson State Park
Brewster, MA 02631
Phone: 508/896–3491

Cape Cod Chamber of Commerce
Junction Routes 6 and 132
Hyannis, MA 02601
Phone: 508/362–3225

About Visiting Fire Island National Seashore

Details About Programs And Facilities

Superintendent
Fire Island National Seashore
120 Laurel St.
Patchogue, NY 11772
Phone: 516/289–4810

Ferries

To Sailors Haven from Sayville: 516/589–8980
To Watch Hill from Patchogue: 516/597–6455 or 516/475–1665

Overnight Accommodations

Long Island Tourism and Convention Commission
213 Carleton Avenue
Central Islip
Long Island, NY 11722
Phone: 516/234–4959

Camping

Superintendent
Fire Island National Seashore
120 Laurel St.
Patchogue, NY 11772
Phone: 516/289–4810

Long Island Tourism and Convention Commission
Nassau Coliseum
Uniondale, NY 11553
Phone: 516/794–4222

Park Manager
Heckscher State Park
East Islip, NY 11730
Phone: 516/581–2100

Park Manager
Wildwood State Park
Wading River, NY 11792
Phone: 516/929–4262

About Visiting Assateague Island National Seashore

Details About Programs And Facilities

Superintendent
Assateague Island National Seashore
Route 2, Box 294
Berlin, MD 21811
Phone: 301/641–3030 (Campground office)

Details About Chincoteague National Wildlife Refuge

Manager
Chincoteague National Wildlife Refuge
P.O. Box 62
Chincoteague, VA 23336
Phone: 804/336–6122

Overnight Accommodations

Office of Tourism Development
MD Department of Economic and Employment
Development
217 East Redwood St.
Baltimore, MD 21201
Phone: 1/800/543–1036
301/333–6611

Chincoteague Chamber of Commerce
Chincoteague, VA 23336
Phone: 804/336–6161

Camping

Superintendent
Assateague Island National Seashore
Route 2, Box 294
Berlin, MD 21811
Phone: 301/641–1441

Assateague State Park
Route 2, Box 293
Berlin, MD 21811
Phone: 301/641–2120

Office of Tourist Development
MD Department of Economic and Community
Development
45 Calvert St.
Annapolis, MD 21401
Phone: 301/974–3517

Chincoteague Chamber of Commerce
Chincoteague, VA 23336
Phone: 804/336–6161

About Visiting Cape Hatteras National Seashore

Details About Programs And Facilities

Superintendent
Cape Hatteras National Seashore
Route 1, Box 675
Manteo, NC 27954
Phone: 919/473-2111

Details About Pea Island National Wildlife Refuge

Manager
Pea Island National Wildlife Refuge
c/o Alligator River Wildlife Refuge
P.O. Box 1969
Manteo, NC 27954
Phone 919/473-1131

Ferries

Director, Ferry Division
NC Department of Transportation
Room 120, Maritime Building
113 Arendell St.
Morehead City, NC 28557
Or call about ferries to Ocracoke from Cedar Island
and Swanquarter, NC Ocracoke: 919/928-3841
Cedar Island: 919/225-3551
Swanquarter: 919/926-1111

Overnight Accommodations

Dare County Tourist Bureau
P.O. Box 399
Manteo, NC 27954
Phone: 919/473-2138

Camping

Superintendent
Cape Hatteras National Seashore
Route 1, Box 675
Manteo, NC 27954
Phone: 919/473–2111

Ticketron, Dept. R
401 Hackensack Ave.
Hackensack, NJ 07601
Or Ticketron outlets in major cities

NC Travel and Tourism Division
Department of Commerce
Raleigh, NC 27611
Phone: 1/800–VISITNC

About Visiting Cape Lookout National Seashore

Details About Programs And Facilities

Superintendent
Cape Lookout National Seashore
P.O. Box 690
Beaufort, NC 28516
Phone: 919/728–2121

Ferries

Contact the Seashore

Overnight Accommodations

NC Travel and Tourism Division
430 N. Salisbury St.
Raleigh, NC 27603
Phone: 1/800–VISITNC

Camping

Superintendent
Cape Lookout National Seashore
P.O. Box 690
Beaufort, NC 28516
Phone: 919/728-2121

NC Travel and Tourism Division
430 N. Salisbury St.
Raleigh, NC 27603
Phone: 1/800-VISITNC

About Visiting Cumberland Island National Seashore

Details About Programs And Facilities

Superintendent
Cumberland Island National Seashore
P.O. Box 806
St. Marys, GA 31558
Phone: 912/882-4336

Ferries

Call the seashore to make reservations
912/882-4335, 10 a.m.-2 p.m., Monday through Friday

Overnight Accommodations

Greyfield Inn
P.O. Drawer B
Fernandina Beach, FL 32034
Phone: 904/261-6408

Riverview Hotel
105 Osborne St.
St. Marys, GA 31558
Phone: 912/882–3242

Camping

Superintendent
Cumberland Island National Seashore
P.O. Box 806
St. Marys, GA 31558
Phone: 912/882–4336
10 a.m. to 2 p.m. Monday through Friday for reservations

St. Marys Tourism Council
P.O. Box 1291
St. Marys, GA 31558
Phone: 912/882–6200

Crooked River State Park
3092 Spur 40
St. Marys, GA 31558
Phone: 912/882–5256

About Visiting Canaveral National Seashore

Details About Programs And Facilities:

Superintendent
Canaveral National Seashore
2532 Garden St.
Titusville, FL 32796
Phone: 407/267–1110

Details About Merritt Island National Wildlife Refuge

Manager
Merritt Island National Wildlife Refuge
P.O. Box 6504
State Road 402
Titusville, FL 32788
Phone: 407/867–0667

Overnight Accommodations

Titusville Chamber of Commerce
2000 S. Washington Ave.
Titusville, FL 32780
Phone: 407/267–3036

New Smyrna Beach-Edgewater
Oak Hill Chamber of Commerce
115 Canal St.
New Smyrna Beach, FL 32168
Phone: 904/428-2449

Camping

Superintendent
Canaveral National Seashore
2532 Garden St.
Titusville, FL 32796
Phone: 407/267–1110

Titusville Chamber of Commerce
2000 S. Washington Ave.
Titusville, FL 32780
Phone: 407/267–3036

New Smyrna Beach-Edgewater
Oak Hill Chamber of Commerce
115 Canal St.
New Smyrna Beach, FL 32168
Phone: 1/800/541–9621
904/428–2449

About Visiting Gulf Islands National Seashore

Details About Programs and Facilities

Superintendent
Gulf Islands National Seashore
1801 Gulf Breeze Parkway
Gulf Breeze, FL 32561
Phone: 904/934–2600

Superintendent
Gulf Islands National Seashore
3500 Park Road
Ocean Springs, MS 39564
Phone: 601/875–0821

Ferries To Offshore MS Islands

Contact MS District of the seashore

Overnight Accommodations

Pensacola Area Chamber of Commerce
Visitor Information Center
1401 East Gregory St.
Pensacola, FL 32501
Phone: in Florida 1/800/343–4321
Elsewhere: 1/800/874–1234

Mississippi Gulf Coast Convention and Visitor Bureau
P.O. Box 4554
Biloxi, MS 39535–4554
Phone: 1/800/237–9493

Camping

Campground Registration
Gulf Islands National Seashore
1801 Gulf Breeze Parkway
Gulf Breeze, FL 32561
Phone: 904/932–5018

Superintendent
Gulf Islands National Seashore
3500 Park Road
Ocean Springs, MS 39564
Phone: 601/875–0821

Pensacola Area Chamber of Commerce
Visitor Information Center
1401 East Gregory St.
Pensacola, FL 32501
Phone: in Florida 1/800/343–4321
Elsewhere: 1/800/874–1234

Mississippi Gulf Coast Convention and Visitor
Bureau
P.O. Box 6128
Gulfport, MS 39506
Phone: 1/800/237–9493
601/896–6699

About Visiting Padre Island National Seashore

Details About Programs And Facilities

Superintendent
Padre Island National Seashore
9405 South Padre Island Drive
Corpus Christi, TX 78418
Phone: 512/937–2621

Overnight Accommodations

Corpus Christi Convention and Tourist Bureau
Box 2664
Corpus Christi, TX 78403
Phone: 512/882–5603 or 1/800/678–OCEAN
Or Texas residents: 1/800/221–SURF

Port Aransas Area Chamber of Commerce
Tourist and Convention Bureau
P.O. Box 356
Port Aransas, TX 78373
Phone: 1/800/221–9198
Texas residents: 1/800/242–3084

South Padre Island Visitor and Convention
Bureau
P.O. Box 3500
South Padre Island, TX 78597
Phone: 512/761–6433 or 1/800/343–2368

Camping

Superintendent
Padre Island National Seashore
9405 South Padre Island Drive
Corpus Christi, TX 78418
Phone: 512/937–2621

Nueces County Padre Balli Park
10901 South Padre Island Drive
Cluster Box 3G
Corpus Christi, TX 78418
Phone: 512/949–8121

Mustang Island State Park
Box 326
Port Aransas, TX 78373
Phone: 512/749–5246

Cameron County Park System
Box 2106
South Padre Island, TX 78597
Phone: 512/761-5493

About Visiting Point Reyes National Seashore

Details About Programs And Facilities

Superintendent
Point Reyes National Seashore
Point Reyes, CA 94956
Phone: 415/663-8522

Overnight Accommodations

The Inns of Point Reyes
Box 145
Inverness, CA 94937
Phone: 415/663-1420

Camping

Superintendent
Point Reyes National Seashore
Point Reyes, CA 94956
Phone: 415/663-8522

Tomales Bay State Park
Star Route
Inverness CA 94937
Phone: 415/669-1140
(Bicyclists and backpackers only.)

Samuel P. Taylor State Park
P.O. Box 251
Lagunitas, CA 94938
Reservations: 1/800/444–7275

Hotel/Motel Chains Directory

For copies of directories of locations of hotels and motels of major chains, write to the addresses listed below or call the toll-free number.

Best Western International
Attn: Travel Guide Dept.
P.O. Box 10203
Phoenix, AZ 85064–0203
Phone: 1/800/528–1234

Day's Inns of America Inc.
2751 Buford Highway, N.E.
Atlanta, GA 30324
Phone: 1/800/325–2525

Econo Lodges of America, Inc.
6135 Park Road
Suite 200
Charlotte, NC 28210–9981
Phone: 1/800/446–6900

Hilton Hotels and Inns
Hilton Reservation Service
2050 Chenault Drive
Carrollton, TX 75006
Phone: 1/800/HILTONS

Holiday Inns
Attn: Directory Dept.
3796 Lamar Avenue
Memphis, TN 38195
Phone: 1/800/HOLIDAY (465-4329)

Howard Johnson Franchise Systems, Inc.
710 Route 46 East
P.O. Box 2746
Fairfield, NJ 07007–2746
Phone: 1/800/654–2000

Hyatt Hotels
Brochure Center
5240 St. Charles Road
Berkeley, IL 60163
Phone: 1/800/228–9000

Marriott Corporation
Marriott Drive
Washington, DC 20058
Phone: 1/800/228-9290

Quality Inns, Including Quality Royale and Comfort
Inns
Marketing Dept.
10750 Columbia Pike
Silver Spring, MD 20901
Comfort Inns Phone: 1/800/228–5150
Quality Inns Phone: 1/800/228–5151
Quality Royales Phone: 1/800/228–5152

Ramada Worldwide Directory
P.O. Box 29004
Phoenix, AZ 85038
Phone: 1/800/2/RAMADA (272–6232)

The Sheraton Corporation
60 State Street
Boston, MA 02109
Phone: 1/800/325–3535

Shoney's Inns
P.O. Box 1260
Nashville, Tn 37202
Phone: 1/800/222–2222

Reading List

In researching background material before our visits to the national seashores, we read numerous government documents, books, pamphlets, and magazine and newspaper articles about these areas. We found still more publications at seashore visitor centers. Many of our readers may want to know more about seashore issues and the areas in which particular seashores are located than we could put in any one chapter. Therefore, we have included a selection of books we think will provide you with many interesting and informative hours of reading.

General Information About The Seashores

Bascom, Willard. *Waves and Beaches, The Dynamics of the Ocean Surface.* Anchor Press/Doubleday, Garden City, NY, 1980. 366 pp. A definitive, in-depth discussion of the dynamics of the ocean surface, both on and off shore. With illustrations, diagrams, and photographs.

Kaufman, Wallace, and Orrin H. Pilkey, Jr. *The Beaches Are Moving; The Drowning of America's Shoreline.* Duke University Press, Durham, NC, 1983. 336 pp. A provocative appraisal of all the elements involved in

the barrier island issue, with specific advice to potential beach dwellers.

Leatherman, Stephen P. *Barrier Island Handbook*, 3rd edition. University of Maryland, College Park, MD,
1982. 109 pp. Written by the Director of the
Laboratory for Coastal Research, this is a professional
presentation of barrier island origins, environment,
evolution, recreational impacts, and development
potential. With illustrations, diagrams, and
photographs.

Toops, Connie. *National Seashores, The Story Behind the
Scenery.* KC Publications, Inc., Las Vegas, NV, 1987.
48 pp. One in a series of soft cover "Story Behind the
Scenery" booklets about various units of the National Park System. A discussion of the geological origin,
the ecology, and the flora and fauna of seashores on
the Atlantic and Gulf of Mexico coasts with many
beautiful color photographs.

Books And Pamphlets Relating To Specific National Seashores

Cape Cod

Beston, Henry. *The Outermost House.* Viking Press, New
York, NY, 1962. 221 pp. A classic chronicle, written
in 1928 of a year-round stay in a house, "The Fo'castle,"
built by the author on a solitary dune facing the Atlantic Ocean at Eastham. From his lonely base, the
author reaches out and absorbs the sights and sounds
of bird, land, and sea creatures, the wind, beach, and
ocean throughout the four seasons, recording his observations and sharing his deeply-felt philosophy of

the relationship between man and nature. Paperback editions: Ballantine Books, New York, NY, 1976 and Penguin, New York, NY, 1976.

Burling, Francis P. *The Birth of the Cape Cod National Seashore.* Leyden Press, Plymouth, MA, 1979, 67 pp. A fascinating account of the crafting of the legislation to create a national seashore on Cape Cod, written by the managing editor of the Cape's major newspaper who was intimately familiar with every step of the process.

Hay, John. *The Great Beach.* W.W. Norton & Co., New York, NY, 1980. 132 pp. A naturalist-author describes the formation of the peninsula of Cape Cod, shows his appreciation of the people who lived and worked on the land and waters of the Cape in the past, and celebrates the Cape as it is today.

Kaye, Glen. *Cape Cod, The Story Behind the Scenery.* KC Publications, Las Vegas, NV, 1980. 48 pp. Written by a park naturalist at Cape Cod National Seashore. This booklet contains outstanding color photographs and illustrations depicting the geology, history, and natural beauty of Cape Cod. One in a series of soft cover "Story Behind the Scenery" booklets about various units of the National Park System.

Richardson, Wyman. *The House on Nauset Marsh.* Illustrations by Henry B. Kane. W.W. Norton & Co., New York, NY, 1955. 223 pp. The keen, sensitive observations of natural events surrounding an old family farmhouse on a bluff overlooking Nauset Marsh at Eastham on Cape Cod. Written by a retired physician who, from childhood, cherished the special atmosphere of the outer Cape. Paperback edition by Chatham Press, Old Greenwich, CT, 1980.

Thoreau, Henry David. *Cape Cod.* Introduction by Henry Beston. Illustrations by Henry B. Kane. Bramhall House, New York, NY, 1951. 300 pp. Also published by T.Y. Crowell, New York, NY, 1972 and Parnassus Imprints, Orleans, MA, 1984. A classic account of the personal experiences and observations made during walks on the shores and through the fields and woods of Cape Cod during 1849, 1850, 1855, and 1857 by perhaps America's most famous naturalist/author.

Fire Island

Bang, Henry R. *The Story of the Fire Island Light.* 1981. 24 pp. Following a brief history of famous lighthouses, the author, a native Long Islander, relates the events leading to the building of the first and second lighthouses on Fire Island and discusses U.S. Life-Saving Service activities on the island. Published in conjunction with fund-raising efforts of the Fire Island Lighthouse Preservation Society, the leading force behind lighthouse restoration efforts. Available from the Society, 99 Maple Ave., P.O. Box P-373, Bay Shore, NY 11706.

Johnson, Madeleine C. *Fire Island 1650s-1980s.* Shoreline Press, Mountainside, NJ, 1983. 214 pp. A historical account of life on Fire Island since the 17th century, including a description of the settlement and current lifestyles of the island's present-day communities.

Assateague Island

National Park Service, Handbook 106. *Assateague.* Superintendent of Documents, U.S. Government Printing Office, 1980. 175 pp. A history of the people and settlements on Assateague Island before the national seashore and an explanation of the major features of a barrier island with color photographs of Assateague Island flora and fauna. Includes a guide to the seashore and practical information on how to enjoy your visit.

Wooten, William H. Jr. *Assateague*, Tidewater Publishers, Centreville, MD, 1982. 58 pp. A history of the people of Assateague Island, including Indians, explorers, early American settlers, and members of the U.S. Life-Saving Service. Illustrated with many old photographs and woodcuts from the late 19th and early 20th centuries.

Cape Hatteras and Cape Lookout

Crosland, Patrick D. *The Outer Banks*. Interpretive Publications, Flagstaff, AZ, 1981. 48 pp. Many beautiful color photographs and clear illustrations accompany this explanation of the dynamics of the beaches, vegetation, and salt marshes of the Outer Banks of North Carolina, written by a staff member of the National Park Service.

McNeill, Ben Dixon. *The Hatterasman*. John F. Blair, Publisher, Winston-Salem, NC, 1958. 288 pp. Fascinating account of the geological and historical forces that have influenced the shaping of the unique character of the people who have lived—and whose descendants continue to live—on Hatteras Island.

Stick, David. *Graveyard of the Atlantic, Shipwrecks of the North Carolina Coast*. University of North Carolina Press, Chapel Hill, NC, 1952. 276 pp. The well-documented story of hundreds of ships wrecked off the North Carolina coast from 1526 to 1945.

Stick, David. *The Outer Banks of North Carolina 1584-1958*. University of North Carolina Press, Chapel Hill, NC, 1958. 352 pp. The geography, history, political, and economic forces at work on the Outer

Banks from the days of early European explorers to the early years of the national seashore. Description of major communities from the Virginia border to Shackleford Banks.

Stick, David. *Roanoke Island, The Beginnings of English America.* University of North Carolina Press, Chapel Hill, NC, 1983. 266 pp. History of English attempts to establish colonies in America. Includes detailed accounts of research and theories about the fate of the members of the Lost Colony.

Cumberland Island

Camden County Historical Commission. *Cumberland Island.* 1985. 16 pp. Short history of Cumberland Island with several photographs of structures and activities during the era of the Carnegie family's residency.

Swinburne, Stephen R. *Guide to Cumberland Island National Seashore.* Eastern Acorn Press, Eastern National Park and Monument Association, Philadelphia, PA, 1984. 64 pp. The author takes the reader on a walk across Cumberland Island from salt marsh to ocean and discusses the island's special complement of wildlife and vegetation. Many detailed drawings of the animals, birds, insects, fish, and shells found at the seashore.

Padre Island

Weise, Bonnie R. and William A. White. *Padre Island National Seashore, A Guide to the Geology, Natural Environments, and History of a Texas Barrier Island.* University of Texas, Austin, TX, 1980. 94 pp. With numerous illustrations and photographs, this guide explains the dynamic natural forces at work on Padre Island and gives a brief history of man's activity on the island. Includes a separate large, detailed, color map depicting the various natural zones and man-made structures.

Point Reyes

Arnot, Phil and Elvira Monroe. *Exploring Point Reyes.* Wide World Publishing, San Carlos, CA, 1983. 146 pp. Point Reyes trails described and classified as easy, moderate, or strenuous hikes. Includes useful tips on preparing for a hike and a directory of services available near the seashore.

Trimble, Stephen. *Point Reyes, The Enchanted Shore.* Coastal Parks Association, Point Reyes, CA, 1980. 32 pp. Through poetic prose and beautiful color photographs, the author explains the enchantment of Point Reyes, its beaches, bluffs, esteros, grasslands, and woods.

Whitnah, Dorothy L. *Point Reyes, A Guide to the Trails, Roads, Beaches, Campgrounds, Lakes, Trees, Flowers and Rocks of Point Reyes National Seashore.* Wilderness Press, Berkeley, CA, 1985. 118 pp. Excellent interpretive, detailed guide for persons who want to hike any of the many trails at Point Reyes National Seashore.

Glossary

AEOLIAN—Windblown.

ATMOSPHERIC/BAROMETRIC PRESSURE—The varying pressure of the air at any location. Usually measured as the height of a column of mercury.

BACKCOUNTRY HIKING—Moderate to strenuous hiking trails in remote, natural settings for the experienced hiker. At national seashores, backcountry camping facilities are primitive (if they are available at all). May or may not have chemical toilets. All supplies, including water, must be backpacked in and out.

"BANKER"—A native of one of the Outer Banks islands of North Carolina.

BARRIER ISLAND/SPIT—An offshore island or spit protecting the mainland and an intervening lagoon or bay.

BARRIER ISLAND/SPIT MIGRATION—The movement along or toward the mainland of a barrier island/spit and its elements (beach, maritime forests, marsh, etc.).

BATTERY—Emplacement of two or more pieces of artillery. Many such installations were part of the coastal defenses of property now within the Florida District, Gulf Islands National Seashore.

BAYOU—A creek, secondary watercourse, or minor river that is a tributary of another body of water; usually a marshy or sluggish body of water. Davis Bayou in the Mississippi District of Gulf Islands National Seashore empties into Mississippi Sound.

BLOWOUT DUNE—A sand dune formed in association with a blowout. (A saucer or trough-shaped depression caused by intense wind erosion of a dune or other sand deposit.) Especially common at Padre Island National Seashore.

BRACKISH—Somewhat salty water resulting from inter-mixing salt and fresh water.

BREECHES BUOY—A canvas seat in the form of breeches hung from a life buoy running on a hawser and used to haul persons from one ship to another or from ship to shore, especially in rescue operations. Used by members of the U.S. Life-Saving Service in rescue operations based on many barrier islands now within the national seashores.

CBRA—Coastal Barrier Resources Act, a law enacted in 1982 establishing the Coastal Barrier Resources System.

CBRS—Coastal Barrier Resources System. Identifies a proposed network of undeveloped barrier units along the Atlantic and Gulf of Mexico coasts where the use of federal funds to aid in future development would be prohibited.

CONCESSIONAIRE/CONCESSIONER—A private individual or business granted the right to conduct certain business services (e.g., transportation or food service) to or within seashore property.

CONTINENTAL SHELF—The undersea part of the wide, gently sloping coastal plain rimming the continent on the Atlantic and Gulf of Mexico coasts.

DUNE—A hill or ridge of sand or other loose material piled up by the wind. May be stabilized (covered with vegetation) or moving (barren).

DUNE BUGGY—Commonly used term to describe a motor vehicle with oversized tires for use on sand beaches; also called beach buggy.

ECOLOGICAL HABITAT—The natural abode of mutually related organisms.

ENDANGERED SPECIES—Various species of fish, wildlife, and plants that are so depleted in numbers that they are in danger of or threatened with extinction. The federal and state governments issue lists of species considered "endangered" and regulations relating to their protection.

ESTERO—Spanish word for tideland, estuary.

ESTUARY—An arm of the sea at the mouth of a river or rivers.

EUSTATIC—Relating to or characterized by worldwide change in sea level.

EXOTIC—Not native; imported.

FAULT ZONE—An area where a fracture has occurred in the earth's crust and one side of the fracture has moved in respect to the other in a parallel direction. Point Reyes is on the western side of the San Andreas fault.

FLOTSAM AND JETSAM—Debris found floating on the sea or washed ashore.

FOOD CHAIN—The arrangement in sequence of prey and predator from simpler to more complex organisms (minnow to fish to fish hawk).

FRESNEL LENS—A lens systems developed for lighthouses in 1820 by Augustin Jean Fresnel, French physicist and pioneer in optical theory. The Fresnel lens creates the intense light beam of a gigantic simple lens by the use of a system of smaller lens sections or units. The Fresnel lens in the Point Reyes Lighthouse consists of more than one thousand pieces of hand cut crystal. Although the light at Point Reyes is now automated, the old light is still operable and can be viewed by visitors to the lighthouse.

GEOMORPHOLOGIST—A scientist who studies and interprets the earth's dryland and ocean bottom surface features.

GLACIER—A field or body of ice formed in an area where snowfall exceeds melting. It moves slowly over a wide area.

GOLDEN ACCESS PASSPORT—Free lifetime entrance pass to all national parks issued to persons who have been medically determined to be blind or disabled and eligible for benefits under federal law. Also permits discounts on fee-paid facilities.

GOLDEN AGE PASSPORT—Free lifetime entrance pass to all national parks issued to persons 62 years or older. Also permits discounts on fee-paid facilities.

GOLDEN EAGLE PASSPORT—An annual pass to all national parks, for which a fee is charged, available to persons not eligible for Golden Access or Golden Age Passports.

"GRAVEYARD OF THE ATLANTIC"—An expression, attributed originally to Alexander Hamilton, to describe the area of the Atlantic Ocean off the coast of North Carolina characterized by dangerous underwater shoals and hazardous weather conditions, where great numbers of ships have been wrecked or lost.

"GREAT BEACH"—Term commonly used to refer to the sweeping beach at Cape Cod facing the Atlantic Ocean from Monomoy Island to Race Point at Provincetown. Also applied to the beach at Point Reyes facing the Pacific Ocean from Tomales Point to the western tip of Point Reyes.

GREENHOUSE EFFECT—The chain of events in which increasing levels of carbon dioxide in the earth's atmosphere trap more of the sun's energy on the surface of the earth, resulting in higher global temperatures, increased polar ice cap melting, and higher levels of oceans.

GROINS—Long, rigid man-made structures extending seaward from the shoreline and constructed for the purpose of blocking longshore currents and protecting the shoreline from erosion.

HAMMOCKS—A fertile area in the southern United States that is usually higher than its surroundings and that is characterized by hardwood vegetation and deep humus-rich soil.

HAWSER—A heavy rope or line used on shipboard.

HURRICANE—An Atlantic basin maritime storm in which winds of 74 miles per hour or more funnel toward a rotating eye or center that moves unpredictably over land or water. Often called a typhoon in the Pacific basin.

INLET—A narrow water passage between peninsulas or through a barrier island leading to a bay or lagoon.

INLET BREACHING—Creation of a water passageway through a barrier island or spit by storm waters.

"ISLAND IN TIME"—A term applied to Point Reyes, California.

JETTY—A structure extended into a sea, lake, or river to influence the current or tide or to protect a harbor.

LAGOON—A shallow sound, pond, or bay communicating with but separated from the sea by a barrier island.

LIGHTERING—The practice of unloading cargo from large ships for subsequent transport in other boats through shallow waters.

LITTORAL DRIFT—Movement of water currents and suspended sand parallel to a shore.

MARITIME FOREST—A natural grove of trees, shrubs, and lesser plants in close relation with and tolerant of seaside conditions.

MENHADEN—A marine fish of the herring family abundant along the Atlantic coast, used for bait or converted into oil and fertilizer.

MIDDEN—A refuse heap.

NATIONAL REGISTER OF HISTORIC PLACES—A national register of districts, buildings, structures, and objects significant in American history, architecture, archeology, and culture.

NOR'EASTER—A storm wind blowing from the northeast. Prevalent along the north Atlantic coast of the United States in the fall and winter months.

"NO-SEE-UMS"—Tiny biting flies so small they are difficult to see. They attack their victims in swarms.

OFF-ROAD VEHICLE/OVERSAND VEHICLE (ORV)—A vehicle designed for traveling off public roads; also called oversand vehicles. Under specified conditions, they are allowed on the beaches of some, but not all, national seashores.

OUTLET—Same as inlet but applied when weather conditions are such that water flows from bay or lagoon through the island to the ocean.

OVERWASH—The over-running of normally dry land by a storm or tidal waters. Applied especially to barrier beaches/islands.

PLATE—A huge, moving segment of the earth's crust which is believed to float on or travel over the asthenosphere, a hot molten layer about 200 miles thick.

PREVAILING WIND—The wind direction that is recorded most frequently during a particular season.

PRIMITIVE CAMPING—Camping in remote, natural areas to which all equipment and supplies have to be backpacked; few or no facilities.

REDOUBT—An earthwork or simple fortification, especially a temporary one, employed to defend a pass, hilltop, or permanent fortification.

REVETMENT—A barricade or retaining wall for protecting earthworks, river, or ocean fronts.

SEA OAT—A dune stabilizing plant that grows on the seashores in the United States South Atlantic and Gulf of Mexico coasts. It tolerates salt spray and its long underground stem and root system anchors sand dunes by collecting grains of sand around its base.

SHOAL—An area in navigable waters that is shallow and hazardous to ships.

SLOUGH—A creek in a marsh or tidal flat.

"SNEAKER WAVE"—A powerful wave that can suddenly emerge from the dangerous Pacific Ocean surf at Point Reyes Great Beach.

STABILIZED DUNE—A dune where plant cover prevents normal wind from transporting sand.

STORM SURGE—The increase in sea level resulting from the low air pressures accompanying maritime storms.

"STREET LEGAL" VEHICLE—A state registered and inspected vehicle driven by a licensed driver.

TABBY—Building material made of lime, shells, and sand or gravel mixed with water.

TIDAL FLAT—An extensive, nearly horizontal tract of land in a very low-lying coastal area that is alternately covered and uncovered with water by the rise and fall of the tide.

TRAILHEAD—The point at which a trail begins.

TRY-POT—A metallic pot used on a whaler or on shore to render whale oil from blubber.

TRY-WORKS—A brick furnace in which try-pots are placed.

WETLANDS—Tidal areas (marsh, swamp, tidal flats), particularly as part of barrier island systems.

WILDERNESS AREA—A federally-owned area defined as an area retaining its primeval character without permanent improvements or human habitation. It generally appears to have been affected primarily by the forces of nature with the imprint of man's work substantially unnoticeable; a place where man is a visitor who does not remain.

ZONE OF CONVERGENCE—(Longshore drift convergence) stretch of shoreline along central Padre Island, near 27° latitude, where southward and northward-flowing longshore currents generally meet or converge.

INDEX

NATIONAL SEASHORES

ABOUT THE AUTHORS: When Ruthe and Walt Wolverton "retired" in 1984, they combined their longstanding interests in nature and travel by visiting each and every National Seashore. The Wolvertons have trekked miles of trails; combed dozens of beaches; studied a plethora of flora and fauna; read a host of history books; and had tons of fun while writing this one-of-a-kind guide. Ruthe and Walt make their home in Severna Park, Maryland.